Will
Smith

Will Smith

by Michael V. Uschan

LUCENT BOOKS
A part of Gale, Cengage Learning

GALE
CENGAGE Learning™

Detroit • New York • San Francisco • New Haven, Conn • Waterville, Maine • London

GALE
CENGAGE Learning™

*I dedicate this book with love to
Madison, Brooklynne, and Maxwell Bates*

LIBRARY OF CONGRESS CATALOGING-IN-PUBLICATION DATA

Uschan, Michael V.
  Will Smith / By Michael V. Uschan.
    p. cm. — (People in the news)
  Includes bibliographical references and index.
  ISBN 978-1-4205-0130-8 (hardcover)
  1. Smith, Will, 1968—Juvenile literature. 2. Actors—United States—Biography—Juvenile literature. 3. Rap musicians—United States—Biography—Juvenile literature. I. Title.
  PN2287.S612U83 2009
  791.4302'8092—dc22
  [B]
                                                            2008050901

Lucent Books
27500 Drake Rd.
Farmington Hills, MI 48331

ISBN-13: 978-1-4205-0130-8
ISBN-10: 1-4205-0130-5

Printed in the United States of America
2 3 4 5 6 7 13 12 11 10

Printed by Bang Printing, Brainerd, MN, 2nd Ptg., 04/2010

Contents

ame and celebrity are alluring. People are drawn to those who walk in fame's spotlight, whether they are known for great accomplishments or for notorious deeds. The lives of the famous pique public interest and attract attention, perhaps because their experiences seem in some ways so different from, yet in other ways so similar to, our own.

Newspapers, magazines, and television regularly capitalize on this fascination with celebrity by running profiles of famous people. For example, television programs such as *Entertainment Tonight* devote all of their programming to stories about entertainment and entertainers. Magazines such as *People* fill their pages with stories of the private lives of famous people. Even newspapers, newsmagazines, and television news frequently delve into the lives of well-known personalities. Despite the number of articles and programs, few provide more than a superficial glimpse at their subjects.

Lucent's People in the News series offers young readers a deeper look into the lives of today's newsmakers, the influences that have shaped them, and the impact they have had in their fields of endeavor and on other people's lives. The subjects of the series hail from many disciplines and walks of life. They include authors, musicians, athletes, political leaders, entertainers, entrepreneurs, and others who have made a mark on modern life and who, in many cases, will continue to do so for years to come.

These biographies are more than factual chronicles. Each book emphasizes the contributions, accomplishments, or deeds that have brought fame or notoriety to the individual and shows how that person has influenced modern life. Authors portray their subjects in a realistic, unsentimental light. For example, Bill Gates—the cofounder and chief executive officer of the software giant Microsoft—has been instrumental in making personal computers the most vital tool of the modern age. Few dispute his business savvy, his perseverance, or his technical expertise, yet critics say he is ruthless in his dealings with competitors and driven more by his desire to maintain Microsoft's dominance in the computer industry than by an interest in furthering technology.

In these books, young readers will encounter inspiring stories about real people who achieved success despite enormous obstacles. Oprah Winfrey—the most powerful, most watched, and wealthiest woman on television today—spent the first six years of her life in the care of her grandparents while her unwed mother sought work and a better life elsewhere. Her adolescence was colored by promiscuity, pregnancy at age fourteen, rape, and sexual abuse.

Each author documents and supports his or her work with an array of primary and secondary source quotations taken from diaries, letters, speeches, and interviews. All quotes are footnoted to show readers exactly how and where biographers derive their information and provide guidance for further research. The quotations enliven the text by giving readers eyewitness views of the life and accomplishments of each person covered in the People in the News series.

In addition, each book in the series includes photographs, annotated bibliographies, timelines, and comprehensive indexes. For both the casual reader and the student researcher, the People in the News series offers insight into the lives of today's newsmakers—people who shape the way we live, work, and play in the modern age.

A "Prince" of Many Realms

In 2006 Will Smith starred in the hit movie *The Pursuit of Happyness*, which tells the heartwarming, real-life story of Christopher Gardner. In the 1980s Gardner went from being a destitute African American father living on the streets with his son to a millionaire stockbroker. In one of the film's key scenes, Gardner's ability to manipulate a Rubik's Cube impresses a rich businessman so much that he gives Gardner the opportunity he needs to become successful. Getting all the colors of one of the confounding cubes to align correctly by continually shifting their sliding pieces is extremely difficult. Many people never try to solve the puzzle because they fear they cannot do it. Fear of failure, however, has never held Smith back from attempting anything he wanted to do. No matter how hard or challenging the task that Smith sets for himself, he has always believed "I can do it."[1]

That strong self-confidence has helped Smith become one of the world's best-known, most highly acclaimed, and wealthiest entertainers. Although most people are lucky to become a rapper, television actor, or movie star, Smith has succeeded in all three types of entertainment. Smith first found fame and fortune as a rapper while still in high school. Although he knew he could continue making money by writing and singing songs, Smith challenged himself by trying to prove he could act, first in television and then in movies. Smith was so talented and hardworking that he was able to succeed as an actor as well as a singer. He has even made the rare transition from performing to producing. Smith started his own company to create record albums, television shows, and films that feature himself and other entertainers.

From Rapper to Movie Star

Smith's climb to fame and fortune began in his hometown of West Philadelphia, Pennsylvania, when he teamed up with Jeffrey Townes to perform rap songs as DJ Jazzy Jeff and the Fresh Prince. Smith was "Fresh Prince," the nickname he got at Overbrook High School due to his fun-loving nature, which made him one of the school's most popular students.

Will Smith's climb to fame began when he teamed up with Jeffrey Townes (left) to perform rap songs as DJ Jazzy Jeff and the Fresh Prince.

Success came quickly to the young rapper. Before Smith graduated from high school in 1986, the rap duo's song "Girls Ain't Nothing but Trouble" was released nationally and become a hit single. And just three years later, in 1989, Smith and Townes won a Grammy for Best Rap Performance for their song "Parents Just Don't Understand." The award made history as the first Grammy ever given in the new musical category of rap.

Smith, however, wanted to do more than sing songs. In 1990 he took the first step toward branching out into another entertainment field when he landed the lead role in the television series *The Fresh Prince of Bel-Air*. Smith was chosen for the part even though he had no acting experience. He got the job partly because he was already famous as a rapper. But his boyish good looks and humorous manner were perfect for the part of a poor young African American who moves from the mean streets of Philadelphia to upscale Bel-Air, California. The show was a hit for six years. Even though Smith's many blockbuster movies since then have dwarfed that show, the series will always mean a lot to him. Smith said in a 2008 interview, "It doesn't matter how many movies I've made, they'll always remember me best for the show. When you're on TV, people are allowing you into their homes. I knew when that show took off that I could accomplish whatever I wanted in this business."[2]

After Smith showed that he could act in the television series, he was able to win roles in movies. *Six Degrees of Separation* in 1993 marked his first appearance in a major movie. He quickly grew more popular, and in 1997 he starred in *Men in Black* and *Independence Day*, two of the biggest hits ever made.

It had only taken Smith a decade after graduating from high school to become one of the world's most well-known entertainers. His rise to stardom was meteoric, and in 1997 Smith claimed that success had come easily: "It kind of developed for me naturally. I started out rapping as a hobby and everything developed from that hobby. I never made a conscious decision that I wanted to be in show business. I was there, I was prepared, and it presented itself."[3]

Smith kept on taking advantage of the opportunities that presented themselves, and in the next decade he starred in hit movies like *Men in Black II*; *I, Robot*; and *I Am Legend*. Those movies all made hundreds of millions of dollars and created fans for Smith throughout the world. In 2007 *Newsweek* magazine claimed that Smith's ability to draw huge audiences to any film he appeared in had made him the most powerful actor in Hollywood, the global center for moviemaking. This ultimate compliment for a movie actor showed that the Fresh Prince of high school, rap, and television had also become a leading member of Hollywood royalty.

Breaking Racial Barriers

The box-office success Smith enjoys has come despite the color of his skin. Many people are amazed that Smith has become one of the world's most popular actors—maybe the most popular—despite the racism against black people that continues to exist in many countries, including the United States. Smith does not deny that racism exists, and he admits that he has suffered from it. Like many entertainers, athletes, and other rich black men, Smith has been arrested by white policemen who were suspicious that he was driving an expensive car.

But the supreme self-confidence that has always given Smith the courage to tackle new areas of entertainment has allowed him to ignore such prejudice. And enough people have also ignored his race to flock to his movies and make him one of the world's most popular stars. Sony Pictures has released some of Smith's biggest hits, including *Hitch*, *Men in Black*, and *Bad Boys*. Sony executive Amy Pascal claims that when Smith stars in a movie, "it doesn't matter what the genre, and it doesn't matter what date the movie opens—people just want to see him."[4] They simply want to be entertained, and they do not care that their favorite actor is black.

Chapter 1

Growing Up Happy and Successful

Will Smith had an unusual childhood for a rap star. Many of the most famous and successful performers in this musical genre have come from broken homes, have gotten into trouble with the police, or have used drugs. Tupac Shakur and 50 Cent are examples of rappers who had troubled childhoods. Shakur never knew his father, his mother was a crack addict for several years, and he was imprisoned for rape. Likewise, 50 Cent never knew his father, his mother was murdered when he was a young boy, and he once made his living selling drugs. By contrast, Smith came from a stable, loving family, and his parents taught him a different set of values than the ones that many rappers acquire while growing up. Smith once explained how his upbringing affected the choices he has made in his life:

> I made a decision not to carry a gun. I made a decision not to do drugs and not to fight, you know. It's not that I lived in such a great neighborhood and that stuff wasn't there. No. I'm a better person than those people [who use violence and take drugs]. I have better parents, maybe, than those people have. It's not geographically where I was located. It's intellectually where I was someplace else.[5]

The intellectual development that shaped Smith took place in Wynnefield, a middle-class suburb of West Philadelphia, Pennsylvania. It began on September 25, 1968, when he was born in Children's Hospital in Philadelphia as Willard Christopher Smith II.

Childhood Lessons

Will was the second of four children; he has an older sister, Pam, and a younger brother and sister, Ellen and Harry, who are twins. Will was named after his father, a U.S. Air Force veteran who owned a business that installed and repaired refrigeration units in grocery stores. His mother, Caroline, was a school administrator who worked for the Philadelphia School Board. When an interviewer once asked Smith who his idols were, he said the only people he had ever idolized were his parents. That was because his mother and father had loved him and taught him the most important lessons of his life.

The Smiths were not rich, but they had enough money to enroll Will and his siblings in Our Lady of Lourdes, a private school. Even though the family was Baptist, Will's mother wanted her children to attend the Roman Catholic school because it was the best one in the area. She did that because she believed deeply that they needed a good education to succeed in life.

Will Smith attends an award ceremony with his mother in 2005. Her choice of schools for her son proved invaluable in teaching him how to deal with white people.

Will attended Our Lady of Lourdes from kindergarten through eighth grade. He was a solid student and brought home B grades. Years later, as an adult, Smith admitted he should have gotten A's. The reason Will did not do better is because he spent too much time making jokes and goofing around with his friends. "I was the fun one who had trouble paying attention,"[6] Smith once told an interviewer. The reality was that Will was so smart that he did not have to work hard to get decent grades.

His mother's choice of schools also proved invaluable in teaching the young boy how to socialize with white people. Until Will started school, most of the people he had come into contact with were black because he lived in an African American neighborhood. But almost all of Will's classmates and teachers at the Catholic school were white. Will encountered some racism from fellow students, and a Catholic nun who taught in the school once called him a "nigger." Although other whites had already used that racial slur for African Americans to hurt the young boy, he was surprised a teacher would use the hateful word. For the most part, however, the whites Will encountered were friendly, and he learned how to get along with them.

When Will transferred to public Overbrook High School in the ninth grade, the racial balance switched again because the students were almost all African American. Smith once said that he learned important lessons by attending schools with both blacks and whites: "For my first nine years, I went to school with all white people. And then I went to school with all black people. So I have a really good sense of the bridge—the racial bridge."[7]

That ability to span the racial divide and appeal to both blacks and whites would become a major part of Will's future success. So would lessons that he learned from his father. Will's dad was a hard worker who believed in doing a job to perfection. One summer when Will was about fifteen years old, his dad ordered him and his younger brother, Harry, to rebuild a brick wall that fronted his refrigeration business. The brothers worked through the summer and after school in the fall and winter to complete the job. The two boys had to tear down the wall brick by brick and then put it back up. Will hated the work because it was hard and the job seemed to be advancing only one brick at a time. But

Overbrook High School students who helped Smith host MTV's Total Request Live pose with him in 2005.

as an adult, Smith explained how proud he was when he finally finished the job and how it taught him about the need to persevere to achieve something he wanted: "Dad told me and my brother, 'Now don't you all ever tell me you can't do something.' I look back on that a lot of times in my life when I think I won't be able to do something, and I tell myself, 'One brick at a time.'"[8]

The self-confidence Will gained from that experience and the loving support he always got from his family made him brave enough to tackle any challenge that faced him in the future. The first challenges came when his life changed drastically after his parents divorced.

Dr. Seuss Influenced Will Smith

Biographer Chris Nickson notes that one of the important early influences on Will Smith were books written by Dr. Seuss, the pen name of Theodor Geisel:

> From the beginning, young Will was quite precocious. Unusually, as Caroline Smith remembered, "He could talk before he could walk," and once he found his voice there was no shutting him up. Each night his parents would read to him, and the Dr. Seuss books became a firm favorite at bedtime, with their nonsense and clever rhymes. They might even have had a subconscious influence on what he'd end up doing as a teenager, as Will noted many years later. "If you listen to them a certain way, books like *Green Eggs and Ham* and *Hop On Pop* sound a lot like hip-hop."

Chris Nickson, *Will Smith*. New York: St. Martin's, 1999, p. 11.

Will Becomes a Rapper

Will's parents divorced when he was thirteen. Although they had always showered their children with love, Will's mother and father had trouble loving each other. They argued a lot, and Will never felt his parents were happy together; when they split up, he was more relieved than saddened. Caroline Smith took her four children to live with her mother, Helen Bright, in a house not far from their old one. Despite the divorce, Will's dad continued to support his children and play an important role in their lives.

The divorce occurred in 1982, at about the same time that Will began going to Overbrook High School in West Philadelphia. Even though Will had been attending a white school, he had no trouble fitting in with his new African American classmates because he had lived in a black neighborhood. His ability to make people laugh helped make everyone like him. Even his teachers admired his joking ways, and some of them began calling him "Prince Charming," which his friends shortened to "Prince." Will later added "Fresh" to his high school nickname; *fresh* was a slang word that meant "new" or "very good." Thus was born the name "Fresh Prince," the name that Will would make famous as a rapper.

One reason why Will fit in at his new school was because he shared the passion other students had for a new type of music that was sweeping the nation. Rap, which is also called hip-hop, began in the 1970s. The first song that became a hit nationally was "Rapper's Delight" in 1979. That historic record made Will fall in love with the new style of music and fired a desire in the twelve-year-old to become a rapper.

Will began making up rap songs and practicing them in the basement of his family's home and with his friends. The lyrics that Will wrote for the songs, however, soon got him into trouble with his grandmother. When Helen Bright read some of the songs her grandson had written, she became angry because they

The Sugarhill Gang performs "Rapper's Delight" in concert. Released in 1979, it was the first rap song to become a hit nationwide.

were loaded with swear words, language that was common in rap music. Smith once explained how his grandmother changed his mind about the type of lyrics he would put in his songs:

> When I first started writing rap, at twelve, I used expletives and four-letter words, because that's what rap was. My grandmother got ahold of my rap book, read it and wrote in the back: "Dear Willard, truly intelligent people do not have to use these types of words to express themselves." We've never talked about it, but from that day on, I didn't use those words.[9]

Rap Music

Rap is one of the most popular forms of music in the United States, with people buying tens of millions of rap albums every year. It is also one of the newest forms of music to sweep the world. Rap, which is also referred to as hip-hop, was begun in the 1970s in New York City by African American inner-city youths. It combines an instrumental background, called the beat, with lyrics sung in an exaggerated rhythmic punctuation that sometimes includes rhyming phrases, alliteration, and words that sound alike. When this new form of music began, it was a way in which anyone who wanted to sing could try to entertain a crowd. As rap's popularity spread, people tried to make money out of it. The first commercially issued rap single was "Rapper's Delight" in 1979 by the Sugarhill Gang. The song became a hit nationally and helped popularize the term *rapper* for someone who made such music. In the 1980s gangsta rap became the most popular style of this new music. The lyrics of the songs focused on the delights of using drugs and having sex and glorified the lifestyles of drug dealers and other criminals. Although rap was based on black inner-city culture, it became popular with many young whites.

Will's grandmother's advice helped shape his performing future because the songs he would make popular were different from those of most rappers, who laced their tunes with profanities. Will started performing the songs at parties and in informal competitions with other would-be rappers, and he later liked to brag that he won every competition. It was at a party in 1985 that Will met someone who would help him achieve his goal of becoming a successful rapper.

DJ Jazzy Jeff and the Fresh Prince

Rappers sometimes have partners. Smith's first partner was Clarence Holmes, whose rap nickname was "Ready Rock C." The two young friends began working together when Smith was fourteen. They soon became so good that people paid them to perform at parties. It was at a friend's party in 1985 that sixteen-year-old Smith met twenty-year-old Jeffrey Townes, who was playing records and singing rap songs so people could dance. Townes performed as "Jazzy Jeff." He had earned that nickname by using jazz records as background music for his rap songs rather than more popular rhythm-and-blues tunes.

Smith liked the style Townes showed onstage. He was so impressed that he performed some songs with Townes at the party. The two young men were drawn together by their common musical interests and a deep friendship that developed instantly. They decided to develop a stage act and began performing at parties and church functions as "DJ Jazzy Jeff and the Fresh Prince." People liked them so much that local clubs began hiring them to play for their customers. Smith sang the lyrics to their rap songs and Townes handled the musical accompaniment, which included playing instruments and scratching records to make strange noises that accented their songs. Holmes sometimes joined the rap duo in the group's early years.

The older Townes had more experience than Smith. He had begun rapping at age ten and had performed with many other rappers before he finally hooked up with Smith. "I worked with 2,000 crews [music groups] before I found this maniac," Townes once said of Smith. "There was a click when I worked with him that was missing before."[10]

DJ Jazzy Jeff (top left) and the Fresh Prince perform onstage in 1988. Smith sang lyrics and Townes played musical accompaniment.

As their fame grew, the two young rappers began to dream about putting out a record. They approached Dana Goodman, who ran a small music company called Word Up Records. Goodman signed them to a contract for one song. Their choice for their recording debut was "Girls Ain't Nothing but Trouble," a comical take on how difficult it is for young teenagers when they start dating. The light-hearted song began with this opening line: "Listen homeboys don't mean to bust your bubble/ But girls of the world ain't nothing but trouble."[11] The song went on to humorously recount the problems Fresh Prince had with several girls he dated.

The record was released during Smith's senior year in high school. Before Smith graduated, he would be a nationally known rapper.

A Hit Song

"Girls Ain't Nothing but Trouble" was such a hit in 1986 that local radio stations began playing it. Eventually it became so popular that Jive Records, a much bigger recording company than Word Up, bought the song and released it nationally. The song was soon playing on radio stations across the country, and listeners bought thousands of copies.

The song's success created a problem for Smith. His parents wanted him to go to college, but he believed his future was in writing and performing rap songs. Even though Smith had not worked as hard as he could in school, he had still been a good student. He once jokingly commented on his high school academics: "I pretty much got good grades in everything. I was bad in certain segments of certain courses. I was bad at dissecting in biology. Touching little formaldehyde frogs, you know, I was really dead with that."[12] What made his choice for his future much harder was that he had been offered a scholarship to the Massachusetts Institute of Technology.

The success Smith was having—and the self-confidence he had that he could continue to make hit records—led him to choose a musical career over college. But when Smith told his parents what he wanted to do, they were unhappy because they thought it would be a big mistake not to go to college. His mother, who valued education, was especially upset. Smith explains their reaction: "I told

Will Smith's Family

In an interview in 1998 with *Rolling Stone* magazine, Will Smith talked about how important his family was to him when he was growing up:

> My mother was this type of woman: When you're learning to drive, you're excited. You hop in the driver's seat, start the car. But mom would stand patiently outside on the passenger's side. I'd say, "Mom, come on!" But she wouldn't move. Finally I'd get it—jump out, run around, open the door, apologizing: "My fault, mom, my fault.". . . My father was the physical disciplinarian. Usually with boys there has to be a threat of physical violence [laughs]. My father made me a soldier, and my mother gave me the strength to be one. . . . I had two sisters and a brother—a team of people to support you. Like my older sister [Pam]: She was an athlete—All-City track—a real overachiever. One time some guys stole money from me and I came home crying. My older sister grabbed a bat and we walked around the neighborhood looking for these guys. I remember thinking, "Damn! This is the person you want in your corner." My older sister always made me feel safe.

Quoted in Nancy Collins, "The Rolling Stone Interview: Will Smith," *Rolling Stone*, December 10, 1998, p. 40.

my parents I wanted to rap. They said, 'Rap?' My mother graduated from Carnegie Mellon. She thought college was the only way. My father could kind of see doing something differently. We agreed that I would take a year making music, and if it did not work out, I would go to college."[13]

His parents let him do what he wanted because they knew he would be unhappy if he did not. But even though Smith decided not to go to college, he still believed education was important. He even admitted once that graduating from high school on June 17, 1986, was one of the greatest achievements of his life. In a

1997 interview Smith was asked, "What's your proudest moment?" He responded by saying, "I have many proud moments. I guess the one that comes to mind most frequently is my high school graduation. I guess it was more a time of pride for my parents, but I felt that it made me feel good and it made me feel proud."[14]

Because Smith was famous as a rapper and movie star by then, that comment reveals a lot about him. It shows that Smith knew his parents had sacrificed much so he could get a good education, and he realized how proud they were that he had finished high school. His feeling good about their happiness showed how

Even though he had become a star with his song "Girls Ain't Nothing but Trouble," Smith says one of his proudest moments was graduating from high school.

much he appreciated what they had done for him. But the love and gratitude Smith has for his mom and dad also extends to other relatives who helped him become the man he is today.

Shaped by His Family

In interviews, Smith has often explained that the members of his family helped him when he was growing up. His siblings always supported him, and he often comments on his grandmother, Helen Bright, for helping him. "Without the things [she] taught me, I would not have achieved my success,"[15] he claims. Smith knows that the love, support, and guidance that his entire family gave him helped him become successful. This is how Smith once explained why that support was so important: "Being there and making me feel better. Telling me, 'Yes, you can do what you want. Go ahead, give it a try, and if it doesn't work, we'll figure that out then; but as smart as you are, it's gonna work.' Once you grow up with that, you can't function without it."[16]

Chapter 2

A Rap Star

I t did not take long for Will Smith to prove to his parents that he had made the right decision by choosing rap over college. On March 18, 1987, Smith and Jeffrey Townes released *Rock the House*. Their first album included their hit single "Girls Ain't Nothing but Trouble" and was a huge success. Fans bought 600,000 albums to give it gold status, a music-industry award for albums that have sold more than a half million copies. The duo's second record in 1988—*He's the DJ, I'm the Rapper*—was even more successful, selling more than 1 million copies to earn platinum status. DJ Jazzy Jeff and the Fresh Prince began performing throughout the United States and in foreign countries such as England, the Soviet Union, and Japan with other rap stars, including LL Cool J and Public Enemy. By the time Smith was twenty, he had made $1 million from record sales and concerts.

Success may have come too quickly for Smith. In a 2007 interview, he claimed that his swift ascent to fame and fortune had some drawbacks. "I had a hit single on the radio for 30 days before I graduated from high school. And that's dangerous," said Smith. "You don't want to have a hit record on the radio when you're in high school." When the reporter asked Smith why he felt that way, he replied, "It just seemed [too] easy."[17] The problem was that he was unprepared as a teenager to handle the fame and wealth that came his way with such early success. And although Smith made mistakes in how he lived and managed the huge amounts of money he was making, the young rapper thoroughly enjoyed his first few years as a professional entertainer and celebrity.

Townes (left) and Smith released their first album, Rock the House, *in 1987 and it quickly sold 600,000 copies.*

Their Own Brand of Rap

Rap was an African American musical style that began in segregated, poor sections of big cities. Blacks used rap songs to explain the hardships, troubles, triumphs, and loves they encountered in their daily lives, including racism from whites. Some of the most popular performers, such as Tupac Shakur, were termed *gangsta rappers*, and their songs glorified criminal activity, sex, and drug use. Many such songs were filled with foul or lewd language, suggested killing cops, and demeaningly referred to women as whores.

One of the reasons why DJ Jazzy Jeff and the Fresh Prince became popular so rapidly was because they were different from most other rap groups. Thanks to the advice that Smith had taken at age twelve from his grandmother, the songs were mostly free of swear words. This allowed them to be played on any radio station, unlike the ranker rap tunes filled with expletives that needed to be deleted. The air play helped their popularity as did the playful, humorous stories the songs told.

A good example of the types of funny songs they created is "Parents Just Don't Understand" from their 1988 album *He's the DJ, I'm the Rapper*. The song explains several of the conflicts that many teenagers have with their parents, such as shopping for school clothes. Young people want to wear smart and stylish clothes while their parents want to buy items that are cheap and practical. Smith sings about a young man who reacts in shock to clothes his mom selects for him, such as a plaid shirt with a big collar. The character in the song argues for nicer clothes, but in the end he has to settle for what his mom wants. His worst nightmare comes true on the first day of school: "And when I walked into school, it was just as I thought/The kids were cracking up laughing at the clothes Mom bought." Smith tells of other situations that can cause tension between kids and their parents, and his constant lament throughout the song is "parents just don't understand."[18]

The song was a hit because its theme is so universal; any teenager, black or white, could understand the plight of the young man Smith sings about. Millions of people loved the song and album, and even Caroline Smith gave her approval. "This album's good," she said. "I can stand to listen to it."[19] More importantly,

DJ Jazzy Jeff and the Fresh Prince

Smith (right) and Townes perform onstage in 1989. Smith credits Townes with inspiring him to become a rapper.

Will Smith would not have become a famous rapper without Jeffrey Townes, his partner in DJ Jazzy Jeff and the Fresh Prince. Townes explains how they worked together to make records:

> We both respected each other's roles so it was very, very easy making records. The hardest part of making records is always coming up with a concept [but] once we came up with a topic then the rest of the song would come within about fifteen or twenty minutes. We would bounce ideas off of each other, I would pretty much do the music and he would lay the rap over the top of it and then we would kind of tweak it. I would say "can we change it and go in this direction" and he might say "can you break it down right here so that we can accent it." It was built on a lot of chemistry, and I've never had that chemistry with anybody else because that came through doing a lot of shows and it was just a natural thing.

Jeffrey Townes, *Jazzy Jeff in the House.* Compact disc. UK: In the House, November 16, 2004.

in 1989 "Parents Just Don't Understand" received a Grammy Award for best rap song. Grammys are awarded by the National Academy of Recording Arts and Sciences of the United States and are the most prestigious honors musicians can receive.

The Grammy that Smith received was a historic award because it was the first ever given in the new category of rap music. Despite their phenomenal success, Smith and Townes were criticized by some fellow blacks who did not like their songs.

Smith Defends His Work

Some fellow rappers criticized DJ Jazzy Jeff and the Fresh Prince for the content of their songs and the style in which they delivered them. Some of their critics disliked their songs because they were too lighthearted and did not showcase the harsher aspects of inner-city life, such as violence, drug use, and foul language. Other people criticized the duo because the themes and lyrics of their songs appealed to whites as well as blacks, which supposedly meant their music was not true rap, which should only be aimed at African Americans.

Some rappers criticized DJ Jazzy Jeff and Fresh Prince because their music and themes appealed to whites as well as blacks.

Ironically, such critiques were aimed at elements of their work that had helped make Smith and Townes popular with a wider audience than many rappers had. Smith was quick to defend his work. He said the humor they put in the songs was an expression of their own personalities:

> We were talking about it the other day, and we realized there is no group like Jazzy Jeff and Fresh Prince. Because what we do is natural, and it runs somewhat, I don't want to say opposite, but somewhat different than the [rap] genre generally dictates. We are silly; we do have fun. Rappers generally don't put that aspect of their personalities in their music.[20]

Smith also rejected the claim that their music was not really rap because its themes had an appeal beyond African American inner cities. He said once, "We want to bring rap out of the ghetto. We're presenting problems that relate to everybody."[21] Critics also said that the problem with their music was that Smith and Townes had grown up in suburban, middle-class neighborhoods instead of the inner-city areas known as ghettos, where life is much harder. Both rappers said they had spent enough time in inner-city areas to know what life was like and that they had been exposed to all of its dangers, but they simply chose not to deal with drive-by shootings and drug-overdose deaths in their songs. Smith told one newspaper reporter that they had experienced the same things other urban teenagers had. "I mean, I've probably seen more people murdered than anybody in the city," Smith declared. "I just happened to be at the wrong place at the wrong time, all the time."[22]

Although such criticism bothered Smith, he and Townes were able to ignore it because they were so popular. They had fans not just in the United States but also overseas. Townes remembers how surprised they both were when they were mobbed by fans trying to enter a radio station in London, England. Townes says, "There was so many people outside the station when we got there that we were like 'What are all these people doing here?' We didn't realize that they were there for us, we got rushed into the station and it took about fifteen minutes to get over the shock of people pulling on us and grabbing on us."[23]

That kind of popularity made both rappers rich. And Smith gleefully began spending nearly every penny he made.

Smith Blows a Fortune

Money began flowing in quickly from albums, concerts, and even a telephone number people could call to find out what Smith and Townes were doing. This was a popular way to find out about celebrities before Internet access became widespread enough to allow people to surf for such information. Smith and Townes made more than $5 million from the telephone service. At the age of eighteen, Smith had more money than he had ever dreamed

A Protest at the Grammys

In 1989 Will Smith and Jeffrey Townes won the first Grammy for rap music—Best Rap Performance for their song "Parents Just Don't Understand." The award was historic and a tremendous honor for the young rap duo, but they did not attend the Grammy Awards to accept it. They boycotted the televised ceremony along with rap stars like LL Cool J and Salt-N-Pepa because they believed the National Academy of Recording Arts and Sciences of the United States was being disrespectful to rappers. Grammy officials for years had refused to recognize rap as a legitimate new music. Even in 1989, when the academy finally recognized rap as a new form of music, it did it in a way that showed officials still disdained rap. There was only one award for rap even though other musical categories got multiple awards. In addition, the academy decided to hand out the award before the televised ceremony began. Smith and other rappers refused to attend the ceremony because they felt the academy was slighting their music. The boycott made officials realize they had made a mistake. It created more rap awards and allowed rappers to appear on television when they received them.

possible. Like many entertainers and professional athletes who suddenly become wealthy, Smith began spending his money as quickly as he earned it.

"I bought everything,"[24] Smith has said. He bought a half dozen cars and a motorcycle for himself as well as a car for his mom. He also purchased an expensive home, clothes, and jewelry, and he spent lavishly on his friends. Smith even took more than a dozen of them along with him when he toured and on vacation so that they could experience the rich life he was now enjoying. Years later, Smith admits that he made a big mistake in how he handled his money:

> I was 18, traveling around the world with more money than I have ever dreamed about. Everything, my entire lifestyle was just out of control. Ten of your friends living in your house playing pool until four in the morning, buying stuff. It's a good thing I didn't do drugs because I can't imagine what my life would be like now.[25]

Although Smith did not use drugs and did not drink a lot, he did succumb to another temptation that is hard to resist for famous, rich young men—sex. Smith slept with a lot of young women in his first few years as a rap star. However, he has said this did not happen until his longtime girlfriend cheated on him. Smith had gone steady with the woman since he was fifteen, but when the eighteen-year-old rapper returned to Philadelphia after touring with Townes, he learned she had been seeing another man. Her unfaithfulness angered and saddened Smith, who had not slept with other women because he had wanted their relationship to be monogamous. Even though Smith continued seeing the woman for three more years, the relationship was never the same because he could not trust her.

Smith began having sex with a lot of other women, which was easy because they wanted to spend time with a rich rapper. When Smith was on tour in different cities, he claims some parents brought their daughters to his hotel in hopes that he would fall in love with them. Smith became addicted to the sex even though the physical encounters felt meaningless to him and made him feel bad about what he was doing. "It was the emotionally darkest time in my life," Smith has said. "It was unfulfilling, but like a drug, you keep feeling you need more."[26] Smith admitted years later that he was grateful he did not take drugs because they might have destroyed him or, at the least, kept him from having the success he went on to enjoy in later years.

When his parents realized that money and fame were changing their son, they tried to talk some sense into him. His father asked him why he needed so many automobiles when he could only drive one at a time. The fancy cars he bought also caught the attention of Philadelphia police. Many black men who can afford to drive nice cars are stopped by white policemen who automatically assume they stole the vehicle. Smith says that happened to him about forty times in Philadelphia while he was

The Humor of His Songs

A major reason for the success of DJ Jazzy Jeff and the Fresh Prince was that people enjoyed listening to their songs because they were so funny. On *Rock the House*, Will Smith wrote a companion song to his hit "Girls Ain't Nothing but Trouble" called "Guys Ain't Nothing but Trouble." The tune notes the problems girls have when they date boys who turn out to be weird, and it has this funny refrain: "So Jazzy Jeff and Fresh Prince don't mean to bust your bubble/But guys of the world ain't nuthin but trouble/So homegirls next time a guy tries to give you the play/Just turn your head and cold diss him and walk away." Fans also liked Smith because he was willing to make fun of himself in his songs. In "Twinkle Twinkle (I'm Not a Star)," Smith denies that he has changed since becoming famous and making lots of money as a rapper. Smith declares that he is still the same goofy guy with big ears—he jokes often about the size of his ears—that he was when he was growing up in West Philadelphia.

DJ Jazzy Jeff and the Fresh Prince, "Guys Ain't Nothing but Trouble." www.oldielyrics.com/lyrics/d_j_jazzy_jeff_the_fresh_prince/guys_aint_nothing_but_trouble.html.

driving his Corvette. "A young black guy with a nice car is going to get stopped, period. And the cops will tell you that,"[27] Smith says. Such stops are racist, and not even celebrities like Smith are immune from them.

Smith has never regretted his brief interlude of crazy spending in his early days as a rapper. In a 2007 interview, he said, "Oh, I had a really, really good time. It was the best blown money ever."[28] What Smith did come to regret, however, was that he failed to pay taxes on the fortune he had accumulated.

Tax Problems

Many professional athletes and entertainers often forget to pay taxes on their income because they are naive about handling such huge amounts of money. One reason why this happens is because they often believe the people who are paying them or their managers are making state and federal tax payments when they are not. This is what happened to Smith after two years of making and spending millions of dollars.

The U.S. Internal Revenue Service (IRS) on February 1, 1990, assessed Smith $2.8 million in back taxes he had not paid. To get the money, the IRS seized many of his possessions and garnished his income, which meant the federal government had the right to take any money he was making to pay for his back taxes. By the time Smith had paid his IRS debt, he was nearly broke. At the age of 20, Smith had made and lost millions of dollars. Smith claimed years later that the IRS debacle was a valuable wake-up call to a young man who was living a dangerous lifestyle: "When you lose all your money you start to focus a little bit. You wake up one day and you can't afford any of the stuff you have. You start re-evaluating your life when all the electricity gets turned off."[29]

Smith's financial downfall was made worse by the lack of success of *And in This Corner*, the third album he and Townes had released. The album was not selling well, which meant that they were not getting big royalty payments. Smith also knew that the apparent downturn in their popularity would affect how much they could make in the future by giving concerts.

Smith's Career Change

It did not take long for Smith to figure out that after all of his early success, he was now in a desperate new situation. "I didn't have any more money," he admitted back then. "So I needed to do more, 'I got to do something [he told himself].'"[30] Smith boldly decided to pursue an acting career even though he had no training or experience in that field. But Smith had always enjoyed acting out the characters he portrayed in his songs while filming videos that were shown on television. So Smith decided to move to Los Angeles, California, which was home to major movie and television companies. Smith left for California just as confident that he would become a successful actor as he had been when he graduated from high school and decided to pursue a career as a rapper. Once again, Smith would triumph more quickly than anyone thought possible.

A Television Star

M any famous singers, comedians, and even professional athletes without any acting experience have tried to use their celebrity to make a successful move to television. Although some of them, such as comedian Jerry Seinfeld and football player Mark Harmon, have succeeded, many have failed to make the transition because they could not act or did not appeal to viewers. But in 1990, Will Smith helped make *The Fresh Prince of Bel-Air* a hit show in his professional acting debut. The young rapper charmed viewers because he seemed nice and acted pretty well, even though he had never done it professionally. Smith once explained why he was able to move so easily from singing to acting:

> I guess the rap records that I made always were almost like theater. The records that I made always had a story. They had a beginning, a middle, an end. I've always had a story sense and I think that the music videos that I made really lent themselves to acting. There's always some level of acting in the music videos. So from the little bit of acting I was doing in the music videos, it opened up the world of live action acting [only a few] years after I had begun performing professionally.[31]

Although Smith's experience in portraying different characters in his songs helped the rookie actor succeed, he was also able to make the transition because he worked hard to learn his new craft. It also

*The TV show **Fresh Prince of Bel-Air** marked the beginning of Smith's acting career.*

helped that the character he portrayed was a near carbon-copy image of himself—a young black rapper from West Philadelphia who moves to Los Angeles, California, and suddenly begins leading a rich lifestyle far beyond anything he had ever known.

Smith's Big Break

Smith got perhaps the biggest break in his entertainment career in December 1989 when he met Benny Medina at a taping of *The Arsenio Hall Show*. Smith had moved to Los Angeles several months

Black Television Shows

The October 2007 issue of *Ebony* magazine listed the twenty-five best black television shows. Author Bryan Monroe chose them from a list of one hundred that had featured blacks in more than six decades of television. *The Fresh Prince of Bel-Air* was ranked sixth, an indication not only of its popularity but also of the effect it had on promoting positive black images. When Smith's series debuted in 1990, the show Monroe picked number one had already been on television for six years. *The Cosby Show* starred Bill Cosby as Cliff Huxtable, the father of an upper-class family whose members are educated, intelligent, and extremely nice, even if they are occasionally a little wacky. The Huxtables were far different from blacks on *The Amos 'N Andy Show* in the early 1950s, who generally conformed to racist stereotypes that blacks were dumb, lazy, or crooked. There had been other positive black shows before Cosby's, but the clever comedian became the most well-liked and respected black who ever appeared on television. Smith's portrayal of a young rapper was nowhere near as powerful as Cosby's Cliff Huxtable, but it helped some white people feel more comfortable with young blacks, even if they hated rap.

before that fateful encounter in hopes of breaking into television. Medina was a Warner Brothers executive who wanted to make a television comedy based on his own life. Medina was born in Watts, a tough inner-city area in Los Angeles. After his mother died and his father abandoned him, the black youth was placed in a series of foster homes. When Medina was finally adopted by a rich white family, he was suddenly thrown into a world of luxury and privilege he had never known.

Medina wanted to update the struggle he had adapting to such a new lifestyle by making the central character a black rapper. When Medina met Smith, he knew he had found the right actor for the lead role in the new show. Quincy Jones, a famed black composer who would help produce the series, also liked Smith when he met him. Medina and Jones quickly arranged an audition for Smith with executives from the NBC television network. It took only a few minutes for Smith to charm NBC entertainment president Warren Littlefield with his easygoing, natural portrayal of the character he would play in the series. "There were no beads of sweat," Littlefield says of Smith's excellent audition. "Will read from a script and nailed it. I just sat there thinking, 'Whoa! Just bottle this guy.'"[32]

Smith's audition was so brilliant that the show's producers patterned the character after him. He would play Will Smith, a hip young black man and would-be rapper from West Philadelphia. After Will gets into a fight with other youths, his mother sends him to live with a rich uncle in posh Bel-Air so he could escape the dangers of inner-city life. The humor in the half-hour comedy flowed from the adjustments a poor inner-city black had to make living with relatives who were wealthy enough to have a mansion and a butler.

Every show opened with Smith singing a rap song that explained why he had moved to Bel-Air and the big changes that it would create in his life: "Now this is the story all about how/My life got flipped, turned upside down/And I'd like to take a minute, just sit right there/I'll tell you how I became the prince of a town called Bel-Air."[33] Smith penned the lyrics and Jones wrote the music for the song, a bouncy tune that added to the series' popularity.

The Prince of Bel-Air

The Fresh Prince of Bel-Air debuted on September 10, 1990. The comedy series would run for six seasons and make Smith a television star. Smith began to realize how important his big break in television was when a famous African American civil rights leader showed up for a taping of the show the first month it was on the air. When Smith saw Jesse Jackson in the audience, he pretended to have a heart attack because he was so excited and jokingly said "Uh-oh, oh, oh, hold on. I know I'm large now—Jesse Jackson is sitting in the house tonight."[34]

Jackson was at the taping because he considered a television show about a young black rapper another breakthrough for African Americans. Jackson had helped blacks win civil rights battles in the south in the 1960s and had continued working to increase respect for blacks in everyday society. Although there were already several popular television shows about African Americans, including *The Cosby Show*, starring famed comedian Bill Cosby, NBC officials had been leery about doing a series featuring a rapper. The television executives had feared white viewers would not watch the show. It was thought that because some rappers had been involved in high-profile incidents involving drugs and violence, whites would not accept a rapper as a television star.

Smith admitted years later that even he had been worried about how whites would respond to a show about a young rapper: "I was one of the first of the hip-hop generation on television, so there was a sense of wonder if it was going to translate, about how America would accept this hip-hoppin', be-boppin', fast-talking kind of black guy."[35] The concerns Smith and NBC officials had about *The Fresh Prince of Bel-Air* were groundless. The comedy was an instant success because of Smith's appealing portrayal of a character that was based on himself. However, it was a success despite the fact that Smith struggled at first as an actor.

Smith Learns to Act

Smith's easy confidence and natural charm helped him give a convincing portrayal of a naive, nice young man from the inner city

The Fresh Prince of Bel-Air

*T*he *Fresh Prince of Bel-Air* featured teenage rapper William "Will" Smith and his California relatives—his uncle, Philip Banks; his aunt, Vivian Smith Banks, his mother's sister; and cousins Carlton, Hilary, Nicholas, and Ashley. During the show's six seasons, Will graduates from fictional Bel-Air Prep and attends the University of Los Angeles. The TV Acres Internet site describes his character:

> Will does his best to fit into an upper-crust family, but he still held on to his street style like greeting friends with his special high five. Besides joking around and playing b-ball (basketball) Will enjoys the companionship of a beautiful female. And being a smooth operator, Will generally has all the right moves to get [dates]. Here are some of the "lines" he laid on his feminine acquaintances:

> Will: Girl, you look so good, I would plant you and create a WHOLE FIELD of y'all.

> Will: Girl, you look so good, I would marry your brother just to get in your family.

> Will: Hey baby, I noticed you noticing me and I just wanted to put you on notice that I noticed you, too.

TV Acres, "TV Character Bios: Smith, Will." www.tvacres.com/char_smith_will.htm.

The cast of The Fresh Prince of Bel-Air *poses for a publicity photo.*

Alfonso Ribeiro (left) performs with Smith in a scene from
The Fresh Prince of Bel-Air. Smith did not think much of
his own acting but the show became an instant hit.

who is suddenly transported to posh Bel-Air. But Smith admits that he was not a very good actor when the show began: "I sucked," he has said, "badly."[36] He also confesses that he was nervous about performing with professional actors. Smith says he was able to do the job by conquering his fears: "On the first day on the set of *The Fresh Prince of Bel-Air*, I was scared stiff. But when I feel like that, I want to attack the fear. That's why I have been successful in things that I've done. I always attack the fear."[37]

The fledgling television star was also able to succeed by working hard to learn how to act. At first, Smith actually worked too hard. He memorized the lines of every actor in every scene so he would know when to speak his own lines. The problem with the memorization was that he unconsciously but silently said the other actors' lines to himself during tapings of the show. Smith says:

> You can look at the first six episodes of *The Fresh Prince* and I was so just hell bent on not failing that I memorized the entire script. And you can see in certain shots [that] I am mouthing the other actor's lines. It took six episodes for someone to tell me to stop doin' it. So then the next six episodes look like, "Ah, come on, Uncle Phil." So I got it together, though. From midway through the first season I got it together.[38]

Smith worked hard to learn to act. He had to know where to stand for scenes so he would be at the proper angle for the camera, how to interact with other members of the cast, and how to use his face and slim, limber 6-foot-2 (1.8m, 6cm) frame—he reached his adult height at age thirteen—to express various emotions. Gradually Smith's performances smoothed out, and he was able to act naturally in scenes with his new family: an uncle who is a rich lawyer, an aunt who is a university professor, and four cousins who are spoiled snobs. His character also has to tangle with the butler, a sarcastic black from England who looks down on the inner-city youth. But in contrast to his often vain and spoiled relatives, Will is a nice young man. He teaches them lessons about humility and how to accept people from different backgrounds. And from them, Will learns how to take responsibility for his life and to get along with people who are richer or more educated than he is.

The show had some critics, including a few African Americans. They claimed the series, whose humor was broad and often juvenile, failed to highlight the harsh life many African Americans faced due to racism. But Smith defended the show, saying it used humor to deal with many of the problems that many blacks faced, such as substance abuse, gun violence, and teenage pregnancy. He also noted that the show brought up a subject that was usually taboo on television and in other media —the fact that rich, educated blacks sometimes look down on poor blacks who are still struggling to attain a decent life. As Smith explains:

> There's always going to be some friction on this show, because it's going to look at something that no other show has—black-on-black prejudice. Everybody knows about prejudice between whites and blacks, but no one ever looked at different types of black people and how they feel about each other.[39]

Smith's character faces such discrimination from his cousins, who have trouble understanding him when he first joins their family because he is so different. The transplanted rapper faces similar treatment from other blacks he encounters when he begins going to a local high school whose students are from rich backgrounds. But Will is usually able to make friends with everybody he meets, and that includes the many viewers the show attracted for six solid seasons.

Smith Kept Rappin'

The increased fame Smith won from the popular television show he was starring in spilled over into rap. In 1991 DJ Jazzy Jeff and the Fresh Prince released *Homebase*, which became a hit thanks to the powerful single "Summertime." The two young rappers worked on the album while Smith was filming the first season of his show. It was easy to do that because Smith had used his influence with producers to get Townes a recurring role on the series as Jazz, his character's best friend.

A Rejuvenated Rap Career

Singers often have short-lived careers because the public gets bored with them. Will Smith's success in television helped keep DJ Jazzy Jeff and the Fresh Prince popular. In 1993, when Smith and Townes came out with *Code Red*, their fifth album, Smith told journalist Jonathan Takiff they were still popular despite criticism of some of their songs:

> We've found that no matter how great you are, or how bad you are, the same amount of criticism will be there for you. It's like Michael Jordan had and probably still has one of the best images in professional basketball. But he takes the same amount of abuse that Charles Barkley does. You know what they say, hindsight is 20-20. That's what we'll wait for, for 15 or 20 years from now, when you look back on the history of rap . . . to get an accurate view of our position. Right now, Jazzy Jeff and Fresh Prince are on uncharted ground. There were a couple rappers who had fifth albums, but never going into a fifth album with the kind of momentum we're going in with.

Quoted in Jonathan Takiff, "Fresh Ink Talks to Jazzy Jeff & Fresh Prince," *Philadelphia Daily News*, October 21, 1993. www.jazzyjefffreshprince.com/interviews/fresh-prince/rapping-with-jazzy-jeff-and-fresh-prince.html.

The album was so well received that it sold more than 1 million copies to go platinum. And "Summertime" won Smith and Townes a second Grammy for Best Rap Performance by a Duo or Group. Even though Smith had to work almost night and day from the fall of 1990 until the spring of 1991 while acting, writing songs, and creating the album, he did not mind the hard work. He told *Jet* magazine about his rigorous schedule that year: "I'm doing the show from nine to five. And from six until midnight I'm in the studio working on the album. As long as I get my eight hours of sleep, I'm fine. I don't need a social life. You see, I've got to work now and I'll have a social life when I'm thirty."[40]

Although Smith's free time was limited, he was not exactly a hermit. His increasing fame and improving financial situation made it easy for him to date and even mingle with celebrities more famous than himself.

Smith Gets Married

The success of Smith's television show made some people compare him to Eddie Murphy, the wisecracking African American comedian who had made it big in movies. Murphy also saw something in Smith, and he called him because he wanted to get to know him. Murphy was one of many famous actors and celebrities who became new friends and acquaintances of the young rapper. However, Smith refused to get too deeply involved in the Hollywood lifestyle, which included constant partying, excessive spending, and a need to follow the latest trends in clothes, food, and other lifestyle concerns. This is how Smith explained his resistance to that lifestyle to one interviewer: "Avocado pizza? You'll never catch the Fresh Prince eating an avocado pizza! I'd rather go to McDonald's. My theory is, just don't try to adjust. When you try to do that, that's when you have problems. Let L.A. adjust to me."[41]

Smith's desire for a simpler, saner lifestyle extended to dating. Unlike some celebrities, who have dozens of romantic relationships, Smith has always liked having a steady girlfriend. When Smith first moved to Los Angeles, he dated Tanya Moore, whom he had met in 1989 while performing a rap concert at San Diego State University. She lived with Smith for a while in his apartment in Burbank, which was near the studio where he taped his television show. When they broke up at the end of the television show's first season, Smith began seeing Sheree Zampino, a fashion designer. He first met her in 1991 while both were visiting a mutual friend on the set of *A Different World*, another comedy featuring young blacks, but they did not begin dating until months later because he was still involved with Moore.

Zampino at first wanted nothing to do with Smith despite his rising fame. But Smith said he fell in love with her very quickly and finally persuaded her to go on a date. Their relationship blossomed after that, and Smith married Zampino on May 9, 1992.

Smith and Sheree Zampino married in 1992. Their first child was born that same year.

On November 11 of that same year their son, Willard Christopher Smith III, was born. They nicknamed him Trey.

A Big New Responsibility

Smith took the birth of his son very seriously. He knew his parents had loved him and that they had sacrificed to give him a good education so he could have a good life. He was determined to shower that same love and dedication on his own children. Smith says that the birth of his son marked the start of a new phase in his life: "When the doctor handed him to me, I realized things were different now." He says he felt the new responsibility for his son the day he took him home from the hospital. "That was the worst drive," Smith recalls. "You're obeying every [traffic] law. You can't be a reckless young man anymore."[42]

Chapter 4

A Movie Star

The year 1992 was a banner one for Will Smith. He was personally happy after getting married and becoming a father, and professionally he was successful as both an actor and a rapper. The National Association for the Advancement of Colored People (NAACP) named Smith and Jeffrey Townes as the year's Outstanding Rap Artists and also chose *The Fresh Prince of Bel-Air* as television's best comedy. Smith says he was able to succeed in two forms of entertainment at the same time by following some advice his dad had given him: "What my father always made very clear to me is just do one thing well, just make sure you can focus. If you do one thing well, everything else will come from that."[43] Smith was able to become a star in two different entertainment areas because he was able to focus on a single task and work hard to accomplish it, whether it was writing and singing a song one day or acting on another.

But even while Smith was becoming a star in rap and television, he was drawn to yet a third form of entertainment. Like almost everyone, Smith had grown up loving the movies. There is something magical about sitting in a darkened theater and watching a film that is so exciting, funny, or scary that it can make a person sit on the edge of his or her seat in anticipation of the next scene. Smith's desire to act in movies came from being awed by how powerfully films affect the people who watch them. He explained once how a film he saw in 1977, when he was nine years old, totally captivated him:

Smith and actress Jada Pinkett appear at a 1999 NAACP event. The two married after Smith and his first wife divorced.

Sitting in the movie theater watching *Star Wars*, I've never had an experience with any form of entertainment that was like that. It was almost spiritual. I couldn't believe that someone's mind created that. [It] felt like [director] George Lucas had a piano that was playing my emotions, and he could go ahead and do whatever he wanted.[44]

Smith wanted to act in movies so he could have that same effect on other people. His growing celebrity enabled him to begin landing roles in movies even though he had no experience in that entertainment medium, which was more powerful and glamorous than the two in which he was already a star.

Smith Breaks into the Movies

His first film was *Where the Day Takes You*, a movie about homeless teenagers in Los Angeles. Smith's first role was a far cry from the heroic characters he would later portray. He played Manny, a

Critics praised Smith's work in Where the Day Takes You, *a film in which he played a homeless wheelchair-bound youth.*

wheelchair-bound youth who is beaten up and thrown out of his wheelchair. Smith was able to make the film during the summer of 1991, after the first season of his television show ended.

The next summer Smith got a part in *Made in America*, a movie about race relations that starred Whoopi Goldberg and Ted Danson. Smith played Tea Cake Walters, the hip boyfriend of actress Nia Long, who played Goldberg's daughter. The film was more prominent than his first one because of its two stars and its controversial topic—the relationship between a white man (Danson) and a black woman (Goldberg) who have a mixed-race daughter. Although the film received mixed reviews, Smith was critically praised for the easy charm and humor he displayed onscreen. It was also the first movie that Smith appeared in that earned more than $100 million.

Smith had worked hard to learn how to become a rapper and a television actor, and he applied that same work ethic to becoming a movie actor. He realized right away that he had to act a new way in films than he did on television. "Everything in movies," Smith says, "is just a touch smaller, a touch slower, because the camera does more of the work."[45] That is because the movie screen is so big and there are so many close-up shots that actors do not have to use the broad movements and facial expressions they do on television. His quick intelligence and willingness to learn helped him master this new type of acting.

Made in America was released in 1993. Smith also appeared in a second film that came out that year, and it was one of the most important movies he would ever make.

His First Big Movie

Six Degrees of Separation is based on a play by John Guare. The movie stars Stockard Channing, Donald Sutherland, and Smith in his most demanding role yet. Smith plays Paul, a con man who tries to convince people he is the son of actor Sidney Poitier in an attempt to get money from them. The part required Smith to express a wide variety of emotions and play two distinct personalities in one character—Paul the criminal trying to get money, and Paul the frightened young black man who is just trying to survive.

In the 1992 film Made in America, *Will Smith talks with actress Nia Long.*

A Prophetic Movie Review

Will Smith was highly praised for his acting in the movie *Six Degrees of Separation*. One of his most glowing reviews came from critic Michael D. Johnson, who claimed at the time that the film marked the emergence of a star:

> Will Smith. Some know him as the "Fresh Prince of Bel-Air," others know him as the rapper, the "Fresh Prince," but for many moviegoers, he's "Paul", the [pretend] son of Sidney Poitier, and he is delivering a memorable and extraordinary performance in the movie "Six Degrees of Separation." Paul [is] played exquisitely by Will Smith. [What] makes Smith's performance extraordinary and memorable is the fact that not only are his acting skills challenged beyond anything the public has seen in his television series "The Fresh Prince of Bel-Air," he at times upstages veteran actors Donald Sutherland and Stockard Channing. This is no easy feat for any actor to pull off. When historians review Smith's work in years to come, "Six Degrees of Separation" is going to be one of those memorable achievements that is discussed and held up as a monumental achievement and break-through in this man's career.

> Michael D. Johnson, "Fresh Prince Delivers Memorable Performance," *Washington Informer*, February 2, 1994, p. 22.

Six Degrees of Separation, starring Donald Sutherland, Stockard Channing, and Will Smith, received critical acclaim.

Smith wanted to be in the film, but Guare and Fred Schepisi, the film's director, both refused to consider him at first because they did not think he could handle such a difficult role. Smith won them over when he finally got a chance to audition for the film. That was the easy part, however, because acting in the movie was harder than anything he had ever done before. For the first time, Smith had to play someone who was much different than himself. But as always, Smith worked hard to master the role by spending eighteen weeks with an acting coach, a dialect coach, and a physical trainer to prepare for the part. In doing so, Smith learned how to really act for the first time instead of just playing another version of himself. Smith says, "I guess, the piece of work that I performed in that shaped me most as an actor and as a person was *Six Degrees of Separation*. The level of the work and the difficulty of the work helped me find out a lot about acting and about myself."[46]

The movie was critically acclaimed when it was released— Channing was even nominated for an Oscar for best actress—and Smith won glowing reviews for his performance. Film critic Frank Gabrenya wrote at the time, "Smith is a revelation, mostly because the rapper and star of television's *Fresh Prince of Bel-Air* proves himself a genuine presence."[47] Smith was no longer a celebrity from another form of entertainment trying to make it in films but a real movie actor.

Many scenes were difficult for Smith because they dealt with complex human emotions involving serious topics such as race relations. The scenes that gave Smith the most trouble, however, were those concerning his character's sexuality. Paul is a homosexual, and in the movie he has several encounters with male lovers. Smith refused to film one scene in which his character kisses a man, so a stunt double did the kiss. Smith later explained why he refused to do the scene: "I just had a new son [Trey]. I didn't feel comfortable with there being a piece of tape that some kid could bring to school 15 years from now and say, 'Your father kissed a man.' It was basically immaturity. I was immature as an actor."[48]

Smith, however, had also been worried that kissing a man would hurt his popularity as a rapper and a television actor. His fears were groundless, though, because the movie's success added to his growing fame and popularity in those media.

Still a "Prince" of Rap and Television

In the fall of 1994, *The Fresh Prince of Bel-Air* began its fourth season with Smith's character now attending college after having graduated from high school. The show was still popular and still funny even though it occasionally dealt with serious issues, such as drunk driving. The series also showcased an occasional rap song by Smith, something that helped him remain a star in the first entertainment medium he had conquered.

In October 1993, when Smith and Townes released *Code Red*, one of the biggest hit singles on their fifth album was "Boom! Shake the Room." Smith admits that the exposure the song got on his television show was one reason it became popular because 20 to 30 million people watching would hear it. James Lassiter, who managed Smith's career for many years, believes the television show helped make Smith popular worldwide because it was shown in Europe, Australia, South America, the Caribbean, South Africa, and several African countries. "Thanks to being on the show," Lassiter says, "Will became an international recording star—something he hadn't done prior to doing the show."[49]

Finding time to record songs and perform them, however, was becoming increasingly difficult for Smith because he was acting so much. He told one newspaper reporter in late 1993, "We'd [he and Townes] like to perform, but I have to do the television show. And I want to do a film every year, like I did this summer with 'Six Degrees.' So time does not allow for touring."[50]

One reason why Smith worked so much was because he had to pay off his $2.8 million federal tax debt; for the first three years of the television show, the government took 70 percent of the money he earned. And in 1995 Smith incurred another big expense, this one related to his personal life as he divorced his wife.

Smith's Personal Life Changes

People who work extremely hard to be successful often spend so much time away from their families that their relationships with their spouses suffer. On December 1, 1995, Smith and

A Learning Experience

Biographer Chris Nickson explains an incident during the filming of *Six Degrees of Separation* in which actor Donald Sutherland taught Will Smith a lesson about acting in movies:

> Within a television series, he could let [his buoyant personality] loose, even on the set, but with a film everything had to be absolutely professional—something he'd learned from Whoopi Goldberg while making *Made in America*. [But there was] one small gaffe as the filming of *Six Degrees of Separation* began. "Will is used to driving the set on 'Fresh Prince' and keeping up enthusiasm," [director Fred] Schepisi recalled. "On the first day, just before a take, he let out some wild yells and clapped his hands. He was deafening the sound people and everyone else around him. Finally, Donald took him aside. It was a way of psyching himself, but once told, he never did it again. "I have this childish energy that manifests itself in noise," Will admitted. "Donald just grabbed my hand [and] said, 'Shut up.' That was cool. I'm totally fine with someone who says, 'I think it's time to work now.'"

Chris Nickson, *Will Smith*. New York: St. Martin's, 1999, pp. 74–75.

Sheree Zampino ended their three-year marriage, and Smith believes his marriage fell apart for that reason. "We had a new son [Trey], and my career was taking off," Smith has said. "There was a lot of pressure that didn't allow the marriage to blossom."[51] Smith was generous with his former wife, giving her $900,000 in the divorce settlement as well as $24,000 a month in alimony and child support.

Children are often hurt the most by a divorce because their parents split up. Smith, however, wanted to remain in his son's life, just as his father had after his own parents divorced. He continued to spend a lot of time with his son and tried to be a good father. One way Smith did that was to punish Trey when he was naughty. But Smith admitted once that disciplining a child can be hard on a parent: "I had to give Trey a spanking for the first time. He cried and I was in the other room crying. It was the worst."[52] He would later write a song called "Just the Two of Us," which he dedicated to his son.

It did not take Smith long to find a woman to love. He first met Jada Pinkett in 1990, during the first season of his television show. Pinkett auditioned for the part of Smith's girlfriend, but television executives thought the 5-foot-tall (1.5m) actress was too short for the 6-foot-2 (1.8m, 6cm) Smith. But in real life Smith did not care about the height difference, and he began dating her in the fall of 1995 after he and his wife had separated.

Pinkett was a successful actress who had appeared in the television show *A Different World* and the movie *The Nutty Professor*. Three years younger than Smith at twenty-four, Pinkett had just split up with basketball star Grant Hill. Smith and Pinkett were friends at first, but they quickly fell in love as they got to know each other better. "For me," says Pinkett, "it was like 'Wow! You are a wonderful guy.'"[53]

Smith and Pinkett dated for two years before getting married on December 31, 1997. By that time, Smith had become one of the world's biggest movie stars.

A Movie Star

His increasing success in rap, television, and the movies created a very nice problem for Smith—deciding which form of entertainment was the one he wanted to concentrate on. Smith once said that he enjoyed all three but that television was the most fun, music the most rewarding, and movies the most interesting. Making films was also more financially rewarding, and the success Smith had in *Six Degrees of Separation* helped him quadruple his salary for his next picture to $2 million. In 1995 Smith starred with fellow comic Martin Lawrence in *Bad Boys*, an action-packed comedy about two half-crazy policemen. The movie was a major hit, and it made Smith determined to quit television so he could act in movies full time.

The Fresh Prince of Bel-Air had saved Smith financially and helped ease his way into making films. But by its sixth and final season, Smith not only wanted to get out of it to make movies but also because he felt the series had run its course. "I felt like it was time to end the show," says Smith. "I wanted to go out solid, while we were still funny."[54] The show's 148th and final episode aired on May 20, 1996.

Smith felt comfortable leaving the show because he had just made a movie that he believed would change his life. Only a few weeks later, on July 2, Independence Day opened in theaters across the nation. Smith had been paid $5 million for playing Captain Steven

Will and Jada

Will Smith once explained to Rolling Stone reporter Nancy Collins why Jada Pinkett was the perfect woman to be his wife:

> There's a lot going on in my mind, things I want in life [so] being my wife is not to be entered into casually. I demand attention because I'm never complacent. With me it will never be "This is where we're going." It's "This is where we are now, but we're going somewhere else." Most women would say, "Can't we stay here a minute?" But I have a sense there's always something greater. Oh, yeah. And you're so much stronger when your partner is strong. I honestly believe that there is no other woman for me but Jada. Of all the women I've met—and there've been a few—no one can handle me the way Jada does. And once you feel someone locked in on you like that, somebody being down for you, there's no competition. And knowing that I'm not going anywhere gives Jada the strength to be what I need. [This] is it. I can't imagine what anybody else could offer.

Quoted in Nancy Collins, "The Rolling Stone Interview: Will Smith," Rolling Stone, December 1, 1998, p. 42.

The actor says his wife Jada, pictured with him at an event, is the only woman who can "handle him."

Hiller, a U.S. Air Force pilot who helps defeat aliens who have attacked Earth. The science-fiction thriller is filled with fantastic scenes, including an alien ray that blasts to bits the White House in Washington, D.C. The movie's most memorable line is voiced by Smith, who asks, "When we gonna kick ET's ass?"[55] The reference is to the hit movie *ET*, which ironically had also been created by producer Steven Spielberg. *Independence Day* was the biggest hit of the year. The film earned more than $300 million, and it made Smith one of the world's biggest movie stars in the world.

From Will to Mr. Smith

The film's success instantly changed Smith's life. More than anything else, people in the movie industry respect an actor who can draw millions of people to films. The huge turnout for the movie's opening weekend had shown that Smith was now one of those stars. In an interview years later, Smith said he saw how it immediately changed the way people treated him:

> It was one of those moments where I just realized my life was changed forever. You know, it was so bizarre. So bizarre, 'cause the *Fresh Prince of Bel-Air* is on, and people scream, "Will! Will! Will!" And on Monday morning, when the box office receipts for *Independence Day* came out, I was Mr. Smith. "Good morning, Mr. Smith. Congratulations." Who the hell's Mr. Smith?[56]

Mr. Smith was Will Smith, the world's newest movie superstar.

Chapter 5

A Superstar

In 1997 Will Smith starred in *Men in Black*, his second straight special-effects-laden science-fiction movie. Some people thought it was strange that Smith was concentrating his acting on a film genre that had rarely featured African Americans. But Smith was simply following a plan he had worked out with James Lassiter, his agent and business partner, to become one of the world's biggest movie stars. Smith explains why he and Lassiter decided he should appear in science-fiction films:

> We got the [list of the] top ten movies of all time, and we realized that ten out of ten were special effects movies. Nine out of ten were special effects movies with creatures. And eight out of ten were special effects movies with creatures and a love story. So *Independence Day* and *Men In Black* were really no-brainers.[57]

Men in Black featured some of the wildest special effects and weirdest and funniest aliens to ever explode—literally, regarding the horrible insectlike monster that Smith destroys at the end of the movie—on the big screen. Smith and Tommy Lee Jones play the black-suited, sunglass-wearing government agents of the film's title. Their job is to keep track of and police a wide variety of aliens who are living on Earth even though humans do not know the strange creatures are there. The film earned $250 million and became a cult classic. More importantly for Smith, the movie reaffirmed his status as one of the world's most popular movie stars.

A Hero for All Seasons

Independence Day and *Men in Black* both earned more than $50 million when they were released during the Fourth of July weekend. Movie studios like to release movies during that summer holiday because so many people are on vacation and can go see them. However, a movie has to be really good to succeed because so many films open for that big weekend. Ever since Smith had the two blockbuster opening weekends, he has liked to brag that he owns that holiday: "There's a piece of me that likes to say 'July 4 is my day, I dare you to stick another movie there.' It's just my job to save the world every summer."[58]

Men in Black *stars Will Smith and Tommy Lee Jones confront aliens in the blockbuster 1997 film.*

www.iamlege

Smith made that comment in 1999 when *Wild Wild West* was released on the holiday weekend. The remake of the popular television western did not fare as well as his other movies, taking in only $27 million the weekend it was released. But Smith rebounded in 2002 with *Men in Black II* and in 2004 with *I, Robot,* which both topped $52 million. And in 2007 Smith proved he was not just a summer hero at the box office. When *I Am Legend* opened on December 14, it earned $77 million to set a weekend record for a non-Christmas film released in December.

That film was further proof of Smith's status as the world's number one box-office star. The film helped him tie Tom Cruise and

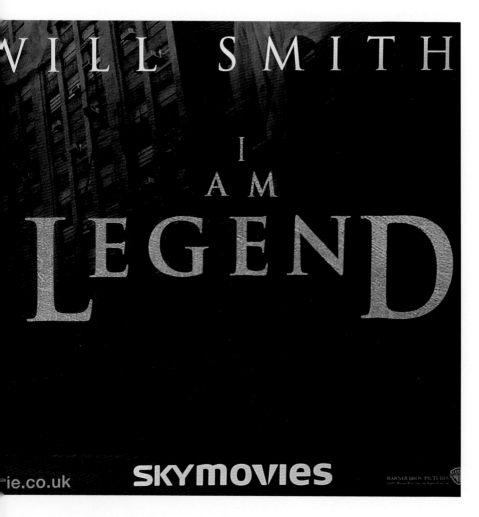

In **I Am Legend,** *Smith plays a character who thinks he is the last man on Earth.*

Tom Hanks as the only three actors in the history of film to have seven consecutive movies that made more than $100 million. But in July 2008, Smith grabbed the record for himself with *Hancock.* The star who rules the Fourth of July helped the movie about the mixed-up superhero sell $66 million worth of tickets in its opening weekend. A few days later *Hancock* soared past the $100 million mark to give Smith eight such blockbuster movies in a row.

Men in Black II's success added to Smith's box office appeal and put him in the same star category as his friend Tom Cruise (pictured).

A Wide Range of Roles

Even before *Hancock* was released on July 2, 2008, movies that Smith starred in had sold nearly $5 billion worth of tickets worldwide. *Hancock* is another science-fiction epic with spectacular special effects that showcase flying, super strength, and other superpowers that Smith's character possesses. Hancock, however, also has super flaws: He is lonely, depressed, and drinks too much. And people hate Hancock because he often damages property or even hurts innocent bystanders with the stumbling way in which he captures criminals or averts disaster.

In one memorable scene in the movie, Hancock removes a dead whale from a beach by throwing it into the sea. His heroic feat is nullified by the destruction of a boat on which the whale lands. Smith loved the strange take on a superhero who becomes a menace to the people he is supposed to be protecting: "Hancock's a horrible superhero! It's one of the most brilliantly bizarre scripts

Smith and longtime manager James Lassiter appear at the premiere party for Hancock. *Lassiter produced the science-fiction film.*

I've ever read. It's actually the dark comedy reality version of what it would be like to be a superhero."[59]

Playing a character who is hated and feared was a switch for Smith, who usually portrays heroic figures. In his first two science-fiction films, Smith saves the planet from angry aliens; in *I, Robot* he fights renegade robots who want to destroy humans; and in *I Am Legend* he is a military scientist trying to save the world's last remaining humans from a virus that has killed almost everyone or turned them into mutant monsters. However, two of Smith's favorite roles were biographies of black men who had achieved greatness—Muhammad Ali and Christopher Gardner.

Ali, which was released in 2001, tells the story of the heavy-weight boxing champion who for decades was the world's most famous athlete. Ali was born Cassius Clay, but he changed his name when he converted to Islam. He was controversial for becoming a Muslim as well as for refusing to be drafted into the army during the Vietnam War. Smith had to train hard physically for the role to strengthen his body, learn to box, and learn Ali's speech patterns and mannerisms.

In an interview in Japan before the film was released, Smith said he was honored to play Ali, who had been one of his childhood heroes. Smith said Ali was a great man who had opposed racism and dared to stand up for his beliefs. "Muhammad Ali," said Smith, "is one of the most famous people in the world. Muhammad Ali is a fighter that made his name in a boxing ring but created his spirit outside of the boxing ring. He is a spiritual genius."[60]

In 2006 Smith starred in *The Pursuit of Happyness*, the story of how Gardner goes from being a homeless man living on the street with his son to becoming a rich investment broker. Gardner is able to turn his life around because he believes that he can realize his dream of having a good job if he works hard enough to make that dream come true. Smith has always had that same belief about obtaining the goals he sets for himself. After Smith saw a television show that explained Gardner's life story, he became determined to play him in a movie: "From the moment I saw the *20/20* piece, I saw this story as the embodiment of the American Dream. The concept this country is based on is the hope that any person, armed with will and determination, can create their

Ali

Will Smith had to prepare harder for *Ali* than perhaps any film he has ever made. Although Smith is physically fit because he is a runner, he had to gain 30 pounds (14kg) of muscle during fourteen months of intensive training to look convincing as the legendary boxer. In this excerpt from a story in *Essence* magazine, Smith explains what he went through to portray Ali:

> Mostly research and study. There was a good seven months that I lived everyday as Muhammad Ali. Director Michael Mann (*Heat, The Insider*) broke down training into a three-tiered syllabus. The first tier was physical, the second the mental and emotional space of Muhammad Ali and the third was spiritual training by Islamic teachers. Generally, I walked around at about 195 pounds [before training for the movie], and I peaked at about 223. We traced why his voice sounds that way (in the mental and emotional sense) back to Baptist preachers who he had seen growing up. That's why he put certain emphasis on words—he would ride up and down and then get dramatic. We found three or four Baptist preachers and I studied the inflection in their voices.

Quoted in Kym Allison Backer, "The Big Will," *Essence*, December 6, 2001. www.essence.com/essence/themix/entertainment/0,16109,266807,00.

For the film Ali *Smith went through fourteen months of intensive training to play the legendary boxer.*

life, can create their situation—from the lowest of the low to the highest of the high."[61]

Smith loved the movie because of the strong, positive message contained in Gardner's life story. But Smith also loved it for another very special reason—his son Jaden starred in the movie with him.

Smith's Talented Family

One reason why *The Pursuit of Happyness* is so heartwarming and touching is because the real-life love that exists between father and son is evident in all their scenes. Jaden Christopher Syre Smith was born on July 8, 1998. Jaden—who is named after his mother, Jada Pinkett Smith—was only seven years old when he made the movie with his dad. Despite his youth, Jaden was widely praised for his acting because he was able to naturally express his emotions in various scenes, including those in which he had to cry. Jaden says he succeeded because he took some advice from his father, who told him to just try to express the emotions he felt while acting out various scenes in the movie: "You have to just be in the moment," Jaden says. "My dad told me to do that."[62]

Jaden is not the only child star in the Smith family. Willow Camille Reign Smith was born on October 31, 2000. She appeared briefly in her dad's blockbuster film *I Am Legend,* and in 2008 she costarred in *Kit Kittredge: An American Girl.* Like her brother, Willow seems to possess a natural talent for acting. "It's really fun," Willow has said of making a movie. "Because on the set, the directors tell you something and you can do it a whole different way. And they will still like it."[63] *Kit Kittredge,* however, wound up putting her in competition with her father because that movie and *Hancock* both opened on the same day, July 2. When Willow was asked which movie would do better, she showed the confidence that has helped make her dad a success by saying her film would attract more people.

Trey has also been involved in entertainment. He served as *Access Hollywood's* special correspondent for events such as Nickelodeon's Kids Choice Awards and the premiere of *The Pursuit of Happyness.* Trey, who lives with his father, also had a guest role in the television show *All of Us.*

Smith starred with his son Jaden in The Pursuit of Happyness. *Jaden's performance was widely praised by critics and filmgoers.*

Although some parents would hesitate to have their children involved in show business at such a young age, the Smiths are happy that their children are following in their parents' career path. "It would be best for us," says Jada. "It's what we know."[64] Jada revisited her acting career when she costarred with Will in *Ali*; in the film, she plays the part of the boxer's first wife.

Jada curtailed her professional life for several years after her children were born, but in 2008 she wrote and directed *The Human Contract*, a movie about a businessman bearing a deep, dark secret. In 2008 Jada also provided the voice for one of the animated characters in *Madagascar 2: The Crate Escape*. She had also performed in the first movie in that series.

A Demanding Father

Will Smith believes a major reason why he has been so successful is because his parents made him feel like he was contributing to the family by making him do chores around the house, like rebuilding a brick wall one summer. Will and Jada Pinkett Smith are trying to instill those same feelings in their children, Jaden and Willow, by allowing them to work in films. Smith explained what he expects of his kids in an interview in 2007:

> In our family we believe successful relationships are based on exchange; that if you are part of a group you have to contribute. They can't just eat for free. There's no feeling like looking in the eyes of a child that knows they're a valuable member of the family. Yes, there are some tough decisions that have to be made, they have to be away from their friends sometimes, but the self-esteem that's created when they know they've done something, added something to the family I wouldn't give it up for anything.

Quoted in Alison Rowat, "A Legend Living Life on His Terms. He's One of Hollywood's Most Powerful Actors. But, Will Smith Tells, He's Not Ready to Trade Movies for Politics . . . Yet," *Herald* (Glasgow, Scotland), December 26, 2007, p. 14.

Will Smith and his family pose for photographers at the premiere of Hancock.

Will Smith's Many Roles

In most movies Will Smith has made he has played a hero, from the alien-bashing Captain Steve Hiller in *Independence Day* to Agent Jay in two *Men in Black* films. Even Hancock is a hero, though a slightly tarnished one. But Smith has also portrayed a wide range of characters in other films, from Manny, the wheelchair-bound homeless teen in his film debut in *Where the Day Takes You* (1992); to Oscar, a jive-talking fish in the animated film *Shark Tale* (2004). Smith told one reporter that he enjoyed making *Shark Tale* because he felt he had so much freedom by doing just the voice for the cartoon fish while not having to appear on screen physically. Smith loves to play golf, and in *The Legend of Bagger Vance* (2000) he played the title character, a mystical caddy who helps a golfer regain the greatness he once had as a player. Some reviewers claimed Bagger Vance symbolically represented God, which would be his most heroic part ever. And in *Hitch*, Smith played Alex Hitchens, an expert in helping other people find dates who has trouble himself finding someone to love.

Despite the acting accomplishments of his wife and children, Smith is still the biggest star in his family. In fact, in 2007 *Newsweek* magazine claimed that his box-office appeal had made him the most powerful actor in the world. Smith shrugs off that prestigious title, but he claims that any success he has had is due to hard work and not raw talent. He once told a reporter, "I've never viewed myself as particularly talented. I've viewed myself as slightly above average in talent. Where I excel is with [a] ridiculous, sickening work ethic. While the other guy's sleeping, I'm working. While the other guy's eating, I'm working."[65]

That fierce work ethic has led Smith to continue to drive himself in other areas of entertainment. He has not only continued rapping while making one hit movie after another, but he also oversees a company that creates television shows, movies, and record albums.

Will Smith—Rapper and Producer

When Smith started being successful in movies, he was often asked whether he preferred making films or singing rap. "Um . . . I enjoy the one that pays the bills!"[66] he responded jokingly. Luckily for Smith, both endeavors pay the bills. In fact, rapping and moviemaking combine to make him even more successful in both types of entertainment.

Men in Black not only established Smith as a box-office champion but also helped him ease back into rap. Smith's recording career had sagged while he had devoted most of his time to making movies. But when Smith sang the title song for *Men in Black,* it became a big hit and won him his third Grammy. He also decided to record a rap album on his own without his old music partner, Jeffrey Townes. Called *Big Willie Style,* it featured the hit single "Gettin' Jiggy Wit It." The tune won Smith his fourth Grammy Award for top rap single. The song was so popular that millions of people began to use the term *jiggy* in their everyday speech. This is how Smith defined that catchy word for millions of people who were not quite sure what it meant:

> Jiggy is the next level beyond cool. Jiggy is when you're cool times 10, like in the [19]50s, the Fonz [from the *Happy Days* television show] woulda been Jiggy. Some people are cool, some people are kinda hot. Some people are kinda sexy. Some people mix all that in one. Not many people can reach that plateau that we call Jiggy-ness.[67]

Not many people can work successfully at the same time in as many entertainment areas as Smith can. In addition to rapping once in a while, sometimes with Townes and sometimes by himself, in the late 1990s Smith helped cofound Overbrook Entertainment with James Lassiter. Their company, based in Beverly Hills, California, has produced soundtracks for *Wild Wild West* and *Men in Black II* and has been involved in some of Smith's biggest movies, from *Ali* to *Hancock* as well as Jada's *The Human Contract.*

Overbrook—which is named after the high school in West Philadelphia that both Smith and Lassiter attended—also created *All of Us*, a television series about African American families who raise their children after divorces; the series ran for four seasons. Will and Jada worked together to create the show, which paralleled their own life—Will's son Trey from his first marriage is a part of their family. Although most of Overbrook's clients in 2008 were members of the Smith family, there were several singers, including the heavy-metal band Wicked Wisdom.

Smith Is in Charge

The main reason that Smith started Overbrook is because he believes deeply in managing his own career. In 2007 he was being interviewed on television when Tavis Smiley, the host of the show, asked Smith if he had made a conscious decision to "really be the conductor of this career." This is how Smith answered him: "Absolutely. I think that—and for artists out there, it's hugely important. You've got to run your career. What happens is a lot of times artists have this talent and they're just looking for somebody to take it and do something with it. And you have to be the creative force."[68]

Chapter 6

Will Smith's Celebrity Lifestyle

In May 2008 Will Smith was jogging near his California home when he came upon three boys screaming for help. They had been throwing a stick into a water-filled canal so their pet dog could retrieve it. When the cocker spaniel became trapped in some weeds, the youngsters became frantic because they feared he would drown. Smith saw the trapped animal and waded into the water to rescue it. The boys thanked Smith, who, before resuming his run, warned them, "Next time you play fetch, play it on the grass."[69] There was nothing dangerous or heroic about the simple act of kindness Smith did for the frightened boys. But when the news media learned about it, they spread the story of Smith's rescue around the world through articles in newspapers and on Internet sites.

The news media reports anything Smith does or says because he is one of the world's most famous people. His success in movies and other fields of entertainment that produced that fame has also made him rich.

Will Smith's Rich Lifestyle

Smith and his family live on a 200-acre (81ha) estate outside Los Angeles that cost some $20 million. That sounds like a fantastic amount of money to pay for a home, but Smith is one of a few stars who earns that much for making just one movie. That $20 million is four hundred times greater than the $50,000 he received for *Where*

With his status as a big-time celebrity, Smith attracts media attention wherever he goes.

the Day Takes You, his first movie. Movie studios are willing to pay Smith that much because it has been estimated that Smith's films average ten times more than his salary, which makes the high-priced Smith seem like a bargain.

How wealthy is Smith? *Forbes Magazine* estimates that he earned $31 million in 2007 from movies, record albums, and his production company, and in 2004 the magazine claimed his net worth was $188 million. Thus, Smith can afford the huge compound he and his family occupy. Their home is 8,000 square feet (743m²), and the sprawling grounds that surround it include a lake, basketball courts, and a pair of par-three golf holes for Smith, an avid golfer.

The large, private estate allows Smith and his family to get away from people who pursue celebrities; even his wife and children are targets because they are famous from their own movies. His home is also a sanctuary from the unreality of life in Los Angeles, the movie capital of the world. Smith realized when he first moved there in 1990 to go into television that "you get lost in Hollywood [the Los Angeles area where films are made]. It's not real [and] not normal by the average person's definition."[70] By that, Smith meant that many people there have so much money and fame or possess such unrealistic dreams of attaining those two goals that their moral values are far different from those of average Americans.

Smith was raised in a normal, working-class community, and his parents instilled in him and his siblings solid values about working hard and taking responsibility for their actions. Although Smith has far more money and possessions than his parents ever did, he is trying to raise his children in a similar manner. The main way he does that is by trying to be a good father to Trey, Jaden, and Willow:

> I have always wanted this lifestyle [of a dad]. Driving them to school and helping with homework, I enjoy that. [For example] Trey loves baseball and likes to go to the batting cages. He's very physical. So my job is to run him around until he is tired and put him to sleep, and then it's time for Jada and I.[71]

Another part of life in Los Angeles that Smith rejects is the high divorce rate of many celebrities. Even though Smith divorced his first wife, he is committed to preserving his marriage to Jada. On May 26, 2008, Smith told television talk-show host Ellen De-Generes that when he and Jada have problems, they talk them out because they want to stay together forever:

> What I found is divorce just can't be an option. It's really that simple. And I think that's the problem with L.A.—there are so many options. So a huge part of the success for [Jada] and I is that we just removed the other options. We're like "Listen, we're going to be together one way or the other so we might as well try to be happy."[72]

Despite Smith's reservations about the celebrity lifestyle in Los Angeles, many of his best friends are also rich and famous. Two of them are, like Smith, among the best-known people in the world.

His Celebrity Friends

Smith still sees people he knew when he was growing up in Philadelphia, such as his rapping partner, Jeffrey Townes. But Smith has met many people since his rise to stardom, and two of his closest new friends are actor Tom Cruise and soccer star David Beckham. They became buddies because they share many interests. One of them is fencing, a sport that all three began practicing.

While promoting *Hancock* in London, England, in June 2008, Smith told a newspaper about the three men's new activity: "Tom has a room for training. We don't get enough time for hanging out, just us three guys, so this is his way of getting together and bonding. David and I go to his home and just do fencing. It's a lot of fun."[73] Even though Smith turned forty in September 2008, he was still very athletic and in great physical condition. In addition to fencing, he has recruited Beckham to teach him how to play soccer.

Smith's celebrity status has allowed him to meet famous, powerful people from many walks of life, including several historical

Even though he divorced his first wife, Smith says he does not believe in divorce and he is committed to preserving his marriage with Jada.

figures. When Jaden was born, President Bill Clinton and his wife, Hillary, sent the Smiths a note congratulating them on their son's birth. And in 2008 Smith was friends with another powerful elected official who won the presidential race that year—Barack Obama. Smith supported Obama's historic candidacy for president in 2008 and has said he would like to play him in a movie. Obama himself believes Smith would be a natural to portray him because they are both tall and share a prominent physical characteristic—large, protruding ears. Obama jokes, "Will and I have talked about this because he has the ears!"[74]

When Smith went to Africa in 2002 to promote *Ali*, he met Nelson Mandela, who led the fight for racial justice in South Africa and became that nation's first black president. On June 27, 2008, in London, England, Smith served as master of ceremonies for a four-hour concert and tribute to the African leader prior to his ninetieth birthday. Smith told nearly fifty thousand people, "Peter Gabriel once said, 'if the world could have one father the man who we could choose to be our father would be Nelson Mandela.' Nelson Mandela has taught us about love and reconciliation, taught us about justice."[75] Smith led the crowd in singing "Happy Birthday" to Mandela.

Smith, along with MTV's Bill Roedy meet with South Africa's Nelson Mandela during a 2002 visit to promote the film Ali.

News stories connecting Smith with such an uplifting event make even more people like him. However, the news media can often produce stories that hurt a celebrity's image, and that has happened at times to Smith.

Adolf Hitler and Scientology

The news media has generally treated Smith kindly. Unlike some celebrities, Smith has never had problems with alcohol or drugs, has never cheated on his wife, and has never broken laws. But everyone makes a mistake once in a while, and in 2007 Smith was criticized for a comment he made while promoting I Am Legend. Smith told a newspaper that every person has some goodness in them, even someone like Nazi dictator Adolf Hitler, who started World War II and killed tens of millions of people in concentration camps. Smith said at the time, "Even Hitler didn't wake up going, 'Let me do the most evil thing I can do today.' I think he woke up in the morning and using a twisted, backwards logic, he set out to do what he thought was 'good.'"[76]

The quote angered many people because they thought Smith was defending Hitler's actions. Smith, however, claimed his comments had been taken out of context because he was only trying to say Hitler was not totally evil. But Smith apologized for the remark, and his image was not greatly damaged.

Some people and media commentators have also criticized Smith because of his religious beliefs. Although Smith was raised a Baptist, he has studied Scientology, a controversial spiritual program created by science-fiction writer L. Ron Hubbard. Smith was introduced to those beliefs by Cruise and his wife, Katie Holmes. Some people condemn Scientology as a cult or pseudoreligion. Smith maintains he is still a Christian—he cofounded the nondenominational Christian church Living Waters in the San Fernando Valley—and not a Scientologist.

Smith, however, defends the right of people to hold such beliefs and has criticized the media for being excessively harsh in their attacks on Cruise's faith. "That's painful for me to see," Smith says. "I've met very few people committed to goodness the way Tom is. But even with different faiths and different beliefs, at the end of the day, goodness is goodness."[77]

The controversy over Smith's relationship to Scientology gained new strength in 2008, when he donated $900,000 to open a private school in Calabasas, California, called the New Village Academy, which his two younger children will attend. The reason for the criticism was that several, though not all, of its teachers were Scientologists.

Such negative news coverage has been rare for Smith, one of the world's most beloved and respected entertainers. Equally as

Will Smith's Religious Beliefs

Will Smith's flirtation with Scientology is one of the few things he has done in his life that has created negative publicity for him. Even though Smith claims he is a Christian and not a follower of that spiritual program, he has been linked to it because of his friendship with Tom Cruise, one of Scientology's most prominent adherents. This is how Smith defended his right to believe in any faith he chooses in an interview with one reporter:

> I don't necessarily believe in organized religion. I was raised in a Baptist household, went to a Catholic church, lived in a Jewish neighborhood and had the biggest crush on a Muslim girl from one neighborhood over. Tom introduced me to the ideas of Scientology. I'm a student of world religion, so to me it's hugely important to have knowledge and understand what people are doing and what the big ideas are. But I believe that my connection to my higher power is separate from everybody's. I love my God, my higher power, but it's mine and mine alone, and I create my connection and I decide on what my connection's going to be.

Quoted in Bob Strauss, *Los Angeles Daily News*, December 14, 2007, p. L6.

rare is the fact that Smith has attained that exalted status despite the color of his skin.

A Black Superstar

Along with Sidney Poitier, Morgan Freeman, and Denzel Washington, Smith is one of only a few African Americans to become top-level Hollywood stars. For most of the twentieth century, racism relegated black actors to bit parts or roles that represented demeaning racial stereotypes. Smith has not only become a superstar in movies but also has been accepted as a heroic figure capable of sav-

Will Smith and Education

Will Smith believes education is important but does not like the way public schools teach children. For several years, Smith hired tutors to teach his children at home. But in September 2008 they began attending New Village Academy of Calabasas, a private school he started with a donation of $900,000. In 2006 Smith explained his ideas about education to *Reader's Digest* magazine, including his belief that people can learn how to do things by themselves:

> The things that have been most valuable to me I did not learn in school. Traditional education is based on facts and figures and passing tests—not on a comprehension of the material and its application to your life [because] the date of the Boston Tea Party does not matter. [I] know how to learn anything I want to learn. I absolutely know that I could learn how to fly the space shuttle because someone else knows how to fly it, and they put it in a book. Give me the book, and I do not need somebody to stand up in front of the class.

Quoted in Meg Grant, "Will Power: Will Smith Is One Driven Guy," *Reader's Digest*, December 2006, p. 90.

ing the entire world. Dawn Taubin is a former executive with Warner Bros., which released *I Am Legend*. Taubin says that people do not care that Smith is black: "You'd be hard-pressed to find anybody with this kind of appeal. He transcends race, gender and age."[78]

Despite his widespread acceptance by white audiences in his rap, television, and movie careers, Smith knows that some people hate blacks. He first commented on how strange it seemed to him that whites could love a young black rapper after his early triumph in television. Smith says, "I meet people every day [to whom] I would just be another nigger if I didn't have a TV show. It's like, 'Well, I wouldn't let just any black guy into my house. But Will Smith, he's okay, he's a good black guy.' That's just something you learn to deal with."[79]

Smith's success has made him a role model for other African Americans. Although Smith enjoys that status, he has admitted that at times being a black icon can be a burden:

It's uncomfortable sometimes because there are so few [black stars] in comparison to successful Caucasian actors. So few that every move you make is "a step for your people." It's like "Wow, that's a bit too much." My only litmus test is "Will my mother be embarrassed by the work I do?" As long as Mom and my family aren't embarrassed, then it generally works out for my people also.[80]

Despite his overwhelming success, Smith keeps striving to reach his goal of being the world's most successful and famous movie star. Smith has candidly admitted his race could stand in the way of doing that. But while promoting *Hancock*, he said he ignores that possible handicap because it could weaken him mentally: "If I say, 'I'm black, so I can never be the biggest movie star in the world, a black person could never be the biggest movie star in the world,' I wouldn't try to be the biggest movie star in the world. I'd be creating a barrier for myself. It rarely crosses my mind— purposely."[81]

Perhaps what makes nearly everyone like Smith is the joy of living that he radiates in the characters he portrays as well as in his own life. Smith has admitted that playing the depressed, negative superhero Hancock was difficult because it is the exact

Extortion and Identity Theft

Many famous people are plagued by people who try to extort money from them or steal their identities for personal gain. Will Smith has been the target of both types of crimes. In 2001 Smith fired Mike Cooley, a former employee. After Cooley was fired, he began harassing the Smiths by demanding money to stop him from talking to the news media about their private lives. He also began following their children and approached them at a local park. When that happened, the Smiths went to court and got a restraining order to keep Cooley away from their children, and he quit bothering the family. In 2005 Carlos Lomax was sentenced to two years in prison for using Smith's identity to get money. Lomax was convicted of fraudulently using Smith's legal name—Willard C. Smith—to open fourteen phony accounts at stores in the Pittsburgh, Pennsylvania, area. He then charged more than $33,000 in merchandise to the accounts in Smith's name. Lomax was already on probation for stealing the identity of former Atlanta Hawks basketball player Steve Smith and running up more than $80,000 on fraudulent credit cards in the player's name.

opposite of his own personality. This is how Smith explained his basic psychological mood to one interviewer: "I wake up every morning based on hope and positive energy, [believing] today is going to be better than yesterday. I feel like my energy is viral. I'm looking to infect people with the positivity that I feel in my heart."[82]

That positive attitude is not quite a superpower, but it has enabled him to become rich, famous, and adored by many people. And Smith thinks that and his other talents could help him accomplish bigger tasks than entertaining people.

Smith's Future

As early as 1999, when Smith was promoting *Willennium*, his latest rap album, he had begun talking about doing something more important with his life. He told one interviewer then, "I just think acting and rapping is a pit-stop. They are something I do for fun but it's too easy for me for that to be my calling. My true calling has to be something hard, and to be able to affect change and leave a mark on the world bigger than [selling] 20 million albums."[83]

Smith and his wife have begun doing something more meaningful by starting a foundation to give grants to young people in the arts. In addition, the New Village School that they established will accept students who cannot afford to pay tuition. Thus, Smith has joined a handful of rich, powerful celebrities, such as Oprah Winfrey and Tiger Woods, who have established their own schools or programs to help young people. And Smith had joked for years that he would like to go into politics and become the first black president. He had still not made that career change by 2009. But the idea that Smith could be elected to high public office is not much harder to believe than the plots of his movies in which he saves Earth from invading aliens.

Notes

Introduction: A "Prince" of Many Realms

1. Quoted in Meg Grant, "Will Power: Will Smith Is One Driven Guy," *Reader's Digest*, December 2006, p. 90.

2. Quoted in Robin Holland, "Will Smith Has Found the Magic Formula," *USA Today*, June 26, 2008, p. E1.

3. Quoted in Will Smith and Jazzy Jeff Fan Site, "Will Smith Interview, AOL Chat 12/23/97." www.jazzyjefffreshprince.com/interviews/will-smith/big-willie-style-chat.htm.

4. Quoted in Holland, "Will Smith Has Found the Magic Formula," p. E1.

Chapter 1: Growing Up Happy and Successful

5. Quoted in Jonathan Takiff, "Fresh Ink Talks to Jazzy Jeff & Fresh Prince, Rappin' with Jeff & Will," *Philadelphia Daily News*, October 21, 1993. www.jazzyjefffreshprince.com/interviews/rapping-with-jjfp.htm.

6. Quoted in Nancy Collins, "The Rolling Stone Interview: Will Smith," *Rolling Stone*, December 10, 1998, p. 42.

7. Quoted in Janet Cawley, "Will Smith: Topping the Charts and Saving the World," *Biography*, July 1999, p. 34.

8. Quoted in Lynn Norment, "Will Smith," *Ebony*, August 1996, p. 39.

9. Quoted in Collins, "The Rolling Stone Interview," p. 43.

10. Quoted in Jeffrey Townes, *Jazzy Jeff in the House*. Compact disc. UK: In the House, November 16, 2004.

11. DJ Jazzy Jeff and the Fresh Prince, "Girls Ain't Nothing but Trouble." www.oldielyrics.com/d/d_j_jazzy_jeff_the_fresh_prince.html.

12. Quoted in Will Smith and Jazzy Jeff Fan Site, "Boomin Back! Pumpin It Up with Jazzy Jeff & Fresh Prince." www.jazzyjeff

freshprince com/interviews/fresh-prince/jazzy-jeff-fresh-prince-red-alert.html.

13. Quoted in Grant, "Will Power," p. 90.

14. Quoted in Will Smith and Jazzy Jeff Fan Site, "Will Smith Interview, America Online Chat, 12/23/97."

15. Quoted in Denise Henry, "Will Smith," *Scholastic Action*, September 6, 2004, p. 21.

16. Quoted in Collins, "The Rolling Stone Interview," p. 42.

Chapter 2: A Rap Star

17. Quoted in *60 Minutes*, "Steve Kroft Interviews Will Smith," November 30, 2007. www.cbsnews.com/stories/2007/11/30/60minutes/printable3558937.shtml.

18. Quoted in DJ Jazzy Jeff and the Fresh Prince, "Parents Just Don't Understand." www.oldielyrics.com/d/d_j_jazzy_jeff_the_fresh_prince.html.

19. Quoted in *People*, "Introducing . . . : Jazzy Jeff and Fresh Prince, Rap's More Mild than Wild Guys," 1988. www.jazzy jefffreshprince.com/interviews/fresh-prince/raps-more-mild-than-wild-guys.html.

20. Quoted in Takiff, "Fresh Ink Talks to Jazzy Jeff & Fresh Prince, Rappin' with Jeff & Will."

21. Quoted in *People*, "Introducing."

22. Quoted in Takiff, "Fresh Ink Talks to Jazzy Jeff & Fresh Prince, Rappin' with Jeff & Will."

23. Quoted in Townes, *Jazzy Jeff in the House*.

24. Quoted in *Ebony Man*, "Will Smith: From Rapper to Dramatic Actor," April 1994, p. 32.

25. Quoted in Will Smith and Jazzy Jeff Fan Site, "Welcome to the Willennium," 1999. www.jazzyjefffreshprince.com/interviews/will-smith/welcomes-willennium.html.

26. Quoted in Collins, "The Rolling Stone Interview," p. 62.

27. Quoted in Chris Nickson, *Will Smith*. New York: St. Martin's, 1999, p. 35.

28. Quoted in *60 Minutes*, "Steve Kroft Interviews Will Smith."

29. Quoted in Will Smith and Jazzy Jeff Fan Site, "Welcome to the Willennium."

30. Quoted in Will Smith and Jazzy Jeff Fan Site, "Ali Interview Japan." www.jazzyjefffreshprince.com/interviews/will-smith/ali-interview.html.

Chapter 3: A Television Star

31. Quoted in Will Smith and Jazzy Jeff Fan Site, "Welcome to the Willennium."

32. Quoted in Cawley, "Will Smith," p. 34.

33. Quoted in Seeklyrics.com, "Will Smith—Fresh Prince of Bel Air Theme Song Lyrics." www.seeklyrics.com/lyrics/Will-Smith/Fresh-Prince-Of-Bel-Air-Theme-Song.html.

34. Quoted in Jeffrey Ressner, "Raps to Riches," *Rolling Stone*, September 20, 1990, p. 45.

35. Quoted in Nickson, *Will Smith*, p. 49.

36. Quoted in Gregory Cerio, "Mister Smith Goes to Stardom," *People*, July 22, 1996, p. 26.

37. Quoted in Henry, "Will Smith," p. 21.

38. Quoted in *60 Minutes*, "Steve Kroft Interviews Will Smith."

39. Quoted in Ressner, "Raps to Riches," p. 45.

40. Quoted in Nickson, *Will Smith*, p. 51.

41. Quoted in Nickson, *Will Smith*, p. 46.

42. Quoted in Cerio, "Mister Smith Goes to Stardom," p. 26.

Chapter 4: A Movie Star

43. Quoted in *Jet*, "How Will Smith Crossed Over from Hit Rapper to Hot Actor," January 27, 1997, p. 10.

44. Quoted in *Tavis Smiley Show*, "Will Smith," December 13, 2007. www.pbs.org/kcet/tavissmiley/archive/200712/20071213_smith.html.

45. Quoted in Nickson, *Will Smith*, p. 66.

46. Quoted in Will Smith and Jazzy Jeff Fan Site, "Will Smith Interview, AOL Chat 12/23/97."

47. Quoted in Frank Gabrenya, "'Six Degrees of Separation'; Class Conscious Farce Jabs Those Who Skate on Thin Upper Crust," *Columbus Dispatch*, February 25, 1994, p. B12.

48. Quoted in Kevin L. Carter, "Daddy Will Smith Does It All: TV, Film, Rap," *Oregonian*, January 2, 1994, p. D6.

49. Quoted in J.R. Reynolds, "'Fresh Prince' a Watershed for Hip-Hop, and African-Americans in General, on TV," *Billboard*, September 24, 1994, p. 39.

50. Quoted in Takiff, "Fresh Ink Talks to Jazzy Jeff & Fresh Prince, Rappin' with Jeff & Will."

51. Quoted in Cerio, "Mister Smith Goes to Stardom," p. 46.

52. Quoted in Will Smith and Jazzy Jeff Fan Site, "Welcome to the Willennium."

53. Quoted in Nancy Mills, "Red Hot Right Now," *Cosmopolitan*, December 1996, p. 114.

54. Quoted in Lynn Norment, "Will Smith," *Ebony*, August 1996, p. 39.

55. Quoted in Will Smith and Jazzy Jeff Fan Site, "Welcome to the Willennium."

56. Quoted in *60 Minutes*, "Steve Kroft Interviews Will Smith."

Chapter 5: A Superstar

57. Quoted in *60 Minutes*, "Steve Kroft Interviews Will Smith."

58. Quoted in Cawley, "Will Smith," p. 34.

59. Quoted in Rachel Gold, "Will Smith's Powerful Performance," *Sunday Telegraph* (London), June 22, 2008. www.news.com.au/dailytelegraph/story/0,22049,23894607-5009160,00.html.

60. Quoted in Will Smith and Jazzy Jeff Fan Site, "Ali Interview Japan."

61. Quoted in Vincent F.A. Golphin, "Pursuit Rolls Against the

Tide of Black Movies to Seek a New Formula for Happiness," *About . . . Time*, December 2007, p. 24.

62. Quoted in Neil Drumming, "Jaden Voyage," *Entertainment Weekly*, December 15, 2006, p. 49.

63. Quoted in Jeffrey Slonim and Jennifer Wren, "Willow Smith: Like Father, Like Daughter," *People*, June 21, 2008. www.people.com/people/article/0,,20208028,00.html.

64. Quoted in Drumming, "Jaden Voyage," p. 49.

65. Quoted in Al Santangelo, "Hard Work Trumps Talent, Will Smith Says," *New Haven Register*, December 1, 2007, p. 2.

66. Quoted in Will Smith and Jazzy Jeff Fan Site, "Will Smith Interview, AOL Chat 12/23/97."

67. Will Smith and Jazzy Jeff Fan Site, "Will Smith Interview, AOL Chat 12/23/97."

68. Quoted in *Tavis Smiley Show*, "Will Smith."

Chapter 6: Will Smith's Celebrity Lifestyle

69. Quoted in Beth Hilton, "Will Smith 'Rescues Drowning Puppy,'" *Digital Spy*, May 19, 2008. www.digitalspy.co.uk/showbiz/a96290/will-smith-rescues-drowning-puppy.html.

70. Quoted in Takiff, "Fresh Ink Talks to Jazzy Jeff & Fresh Prince, Rappin' with Jeff & Will."

71. Quoted in Will Smith and Jazzy Jeff Fan Site, "Welcome to the Willennium."

72. Quoted in Rennie Dyball, "Will Smith: 'Divorce Is Not an Option,'" *People*, May 27, 2008. www.people.com/people/article/0,,20202478,00.html.

73. Quoted in *Daily Mirror* (England), "Tom Cruise Introduces David Beckham and Will Smith to Fencing," June 20, 2008. www.mirror.co.uk/showbiz/frontpageshowbiz/2008/06/20/tom-cruise-introduces-david-beckham-and-will-smith-to-fencing-89520-20614133.

74. Quoted in *Huffington Post*, "Obama Would Pick Will Smith to Play Him in Movie: 'He Has the Ears!'" February 25, 2008.

www.huffingtonpost.com/2008/02/25/obama-would-pick-will-smi_n_88405.html.

75. Quoted in Mike Collett-White, "Will Smith Kicks Off Nelson Mandela Birthday Gig," June 27, 2008. http://africa. reuters.com/wire/news/usnL2741787.html.

76. Quoted in Dave Goldiner, "I Am Clueless: Even Hitler Not Pure Evil, Says Smith," *New York Daily News*, December 25, 2007, p. 2.

77. Quoted in Holland, "Will Smith Has Found the Magic Formula," p. E1.

78. Quoted in John Horn and Chris Lee, "He Is Legend; Will Smith Breaks the Belief That a Young Black Actor Can't Be Hollywood's Leading Man," *Baltimore Sun*, December 20, 2007, p. C5.

79. Quoted in Nickson, *Will Smith*, p. 70.

80. Quoted in Cawley, "Will Smith," p. 34.

81. Quoted in Horn and Lee, "He Is Legend," p. C5.

82. Quoted in *Tavis Smiley Show*, "Will Smith."

83. Quoted in Will Smith and Jazzy Jeff Fan Site, "Welcome to the Willennium."

Important Dates

1968

Willard Christopher Smith II is born on September 25, 1968, in Philadelphia, Pennsylvania.

1981

Twelve-year-old Smith becomes interested in rap music.

1982

On August 20 Smith begins attending Overbrook High School.

1986

Will Smith and Jeffrey Townes release the hit single "Girls Ain't Nothing but Trouble"; on June 17 Smith graduates from Overbrook High School.

1987

On March 18 Smith and Townes release *Rock the House*.

1990

On Feburary 1 the Internal Revenue Service assesses Smith $2.8 million in back taxes. On September 10 the television series *The Fresh Prince of Bel-Air* debuts; it is a hit and runs through May 20, 1996.

1991

On July 23 Smith releases *Homebase*; the hit single "Summertime" wins a Grammy for Best Rap Performance by a Duo or Group.

1992

On May 9 Smith marries Sheree Zampino; on November 11 they have a son, Willard Christopher Smith III (nicknamed "Trey").

1996

On July 2 the blockbuster movie *Independence Day* opens and makes Smith a major movie star.

1997

On July 2 *Men in Black* opens. On November 25 Smith releases *Big Willie Style*, his first solo album. On December 31, Smith marries Jada Pinkett.

1998

In February Smith wins his first solo Grammy Award for Best Rap Solo Performance for *Men In Black*. Jaden Christopher Syre Smith is born on July 8.

1999

On November 16 Smith releases *Willennium*.

2000

Willow Camille Reign Smith is born on October 31.

2001

On December 25 *Ali* is released.

2004

I, Robot is released on July 16.

2006

On December 15 *The Pursuit of Happyness* is released.

2007

I Am Legend premieres on December 14.

2008

On July 2 *Hancock* is released.

For More Information

Books

Jan Berenson, *Will Power! A Biography of Will Smith*. New York: Simon Spotlight Entertainment, 1997. A biography for the younger reader.

Will Smith, *Just the Two of Us*. New York: Scholastic, 2001. A picture book based on a song Smith wrote about being a father.

Web Sites

The Fresh Prince of Bel-Air (www.tv.com/fresh-prince-of-bel-air/show/475/summary.html). This TV.com site summarizes plots of the show's episodes and has other information on the series, including photographs, videos, and links to other relevant sites.

Internet Movie Database (www.imdb.com/name/nm0000226). This site contains lists of movies Will Smith has made, pictures, a biography, news stories, and links to other sites about him.

The Official Will Smith Website (www.willsmith.net). This site includes news about Will Smith's movies and music, photographs, Internet links, and sound files.

Overbrook Entertainment (www.overbrookent.com). The Internet site for the production company Will Smith cofounded includes information on current projects, photographs, videos, and links to sites connected to those projects.

Will Smith and Jazzy Jeff Fan Site (www.jazzyjefffreshprince.com). This site offers information about Jazzy Jeff and the Fresh Prince as well as links to other sites.

Picture Credits

Cover, Stephen Shugerman/Getty Images
© Photos12/Alamy, 54
AP Images, 9, 37
© Bureau L.A. Collection/Corbis, 51
© Stephanie Cardinale/People Avenue/Corbis, 13
© Reuters/Corbis, 81
Claire Greenway/Getty Images, 64–65
Scott Gries/Getty Images, 15
Naashon Zalk/Getty Images, 82–83
Issei Kato/AFP/Getty Images, 78
David Drapkin/Image Direct/Getty Images, 26
Michael Ochs Archives/Getty Images, 28
Al Pereira/Michael Ochs Archives/Getty Images, 20
Miranda Shen/Photos International/Getty Images, 47
Ron Wolfson/Time-Life Pictures/Getty Images, 29
Michael Caulfield/Wire Image/Getty Images, 17
Lester Cohen/Wire Image/Getty Images, 73
Eric Charbonneau/LeStudio/Wire Image/Getty Images, 67
Chris Pizzello/Landov, 66
Rose Prouser/Reuters/Landov, 50
Reuters/Landov, 63
Geraldo Somuza/Landov, 60
Columbia/The Kobal Collection/Conner, Frank/The Picture
    Desk Inc., 69
Columbia/The Kobal Collection/Rosenthal, Zade/The Picture
    Desk Inc., 71
NBC/Stuffed Dog/Quincy Jones/ENT/The Kobal Collection/The
    Picture Desk Inc., 23, 41, 42
Warner Bros./The Kobal Collection/The Picture Desk Inc., 53

Michael V. Uschan has written nearly seventy books, including *Life of an American Soldier in Iraq*, for which he won the 2005 Council for Wisconsin Writers Juvenile Nonfiction Award. It was the second time that he has won the award. Mr. Uschan began his career as a writer and editor with United Press International, a wire service that provided stories to newspapers, radio, and television. Journalism is sometimes called "history in a hurry." Mr. Uschan considers writing history books a natural extension of the skills he developed in his many years as a journalist. He and his wife, Barbara, reside in the Milwaukee suburb of Franklin, Wisconsin.